Spreadsheets

with Excel

Learning Made Simple

Stephen Morris

ELSEVIER

AMSTERD
PARIS •

Butterworth-Heinemann is an imprint of Elsevier

BH

Butterworth-Heinemann is an imprint of Elsevier
Linacre House, Jordan Hill, Oxford OX2 8DP, UK
30 Corporate Drive, Suite 400, Burlington, MA 01803, USA

First edition 2006

British Library Cataloging in Publication Data
A catalogue record for this book is available from the British Library

Library of Congress Cataloging in Publication Data
A catalogue record for this book is available from the Library of Congress

ISBN-13: 978-0-7506-8185-8
ISBN-10: 0-7506-8185-3

For information on all Made Simple publications
visit our website at http://books.elsevier.com

Typeset by Butford Technical Publishing Ltd, Birlingham, Worcs.
Printed and bound in Italy

Contents

9   Macros   109

Preface

The books in the Learning Made Simple series aim to do exactly what it says on the cover – make learning simple.

A Learning Made Simple book:

◆ Is **fully illustrated**: with clearly labelled screenshots.

◆ Is **easy to read**: with brief explanations, and clear instructions.

◆ Is **task-based**: each short section concentrates on one job at a time.

◆ **Builds knowledge**: ideas and techniques are presented in the right order so that your understanding builds progressively as you work through the book.

◆ Is **flexible**: as each section is self-contained, if you know it, you can skip it.

The books in the Learning Made Simple books series are designed with learning in mind, and so do not directly follow the structure of any specific syllabus – but they do cover the content. This book covers Module 4 of the ECDL syllabus and the Spreadsheets and Graphs aspects of New CLAIT. For details of how the sections map against your syllabus, please go to the website:

http://www.madesimple.co.uk

Acknowledgments

I would like to thank Natalia Żak for her hard work during the production of this book.

1 First steps

About Excel

The Excel spreadsheet program lets you manage all types of information, whether for business or personal use. The program can process data from many sources: ranging from mainly numeric tables – such as balance sheets, sales returns and production schedules – to the sort of lists more usually associated with database programs. This book shows you how to handle this information and make the most of Excel's facilities.

Basic steps

- **To get Excel up and running**

1 Click on the Windows **Start** button, in the bottom left-hand corner of the screen.

2 Select the **All Programs** option.

3 Select **Microsoft Office** from the list.

4 Select **Microsoft Office Excel 2003**.

The program is loaded and the Excel display will take up most of the screen.

Alternatively, copy the Excel shortcut to the Desktop or a folder on the Desktop, then double-click on the Excel icon.

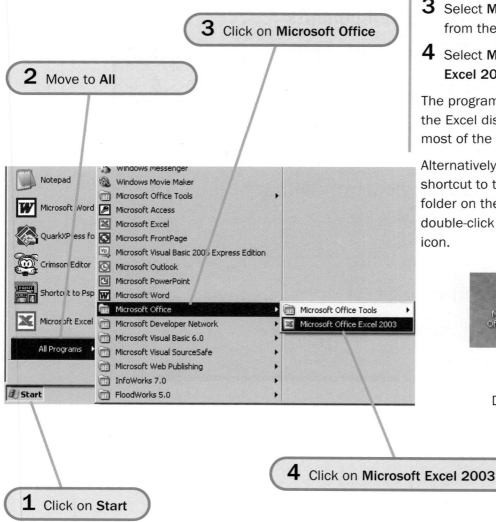

3 Click on **Microsoft Office**

2 Move to **All**

1 Click on **Start**

4 Click on **Microsoft Excel 2003**

Double-click to run Excel

Components

- The **title bar** tells you the title of the file.

- The **menu bar** has a set of drop-down menus giving access to Excel's features.

- The **toolbar** is a row of buttons and selection boxes which provide shortcuts to the menu options or quick ways of entering values.

- The **sheet tabs** and **tab buttons** let you move from one worksheet to another (see **pages 78 and 81**).

- The **scroll bars** allow fast movement within a sheet.

- The **status bar** displays messages and gives information, such as whether [**Num Lock**] is switched on.

- The **task pane** lists suggestions for possible actions.

- The main **grid** is where data is entered, and results displayed.

Screen components

Excel runs under all recent versions of Windows, making the most of its mouse and icon based options. However, in common with most modern Windows applications, Excel provides a screen that is extremely cluttered and can be very daunting to the new user. In fact, you may never use many of the options that are presented to you and you will quickly find and master the most useful ones.

The main components of the display are listed briefly here, with fuller descriptions given later.

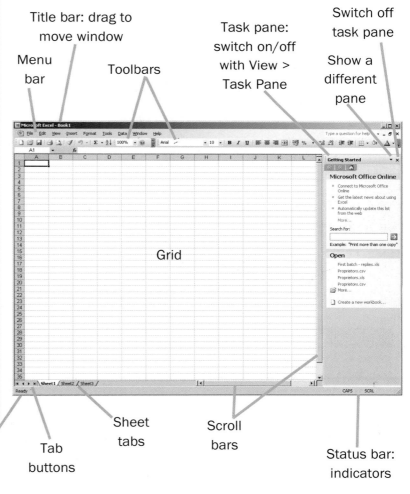

Title bar: drag to move window

Menu bar

Toolbars

Task pane: switch on/off with View > Task Pane

Switch off task pane

Show a different pane

Grid

Tab buttons

Sheet tabs

Scroll bars

Status bar: indicators

Status bar: messages

3

The worksheet grid

In common with all other spreadsheet programs, Excel is organised around a simple grid system. The grid consists of a rectangular array of **rows** and **columns** and is called a **worksheet**. The columns are labelled with letters: A, B, C and so on; the rows are numbered from 1 down the sheet.

The intersection of each row and column forms a **cell**. Any item of data entered on the sheet is placed in one of these cells; each cell can hold one and only one item of data.

The cells are identified by combining the cell letter and row number (the **cell reference**). For example, the cell in the top left-hand corner of the sheet is A1. To the right of this is B1, then C1, and so on. The cells in the second row are labelled A2, B2, C2, etc.

Limits

Excel allows you to create very large worksheets.

■ The first 26 columns are labelled A to Z, the next 26 are AA to AZ, then BA to BZ, and so on up to column IV (giving 256 columns in all).

■ The rows are numbered from 1 to 65,536, giving over 16 million cells.

However, spreadsheets become unmanageable if they get too large.

	A	B	C	D	E	F	G	H
1	A1	B1	C1					
2	A2	B2	C2					
3								
4								
5				D5				H5
6								
7								
8								
9								
10								
11								
12							G12	
13								
14								
15						F15		
16								
17								

Microsoft Excel - Book1

File   Edit   View   Insert   Format   Tools   Data   Window   Help

A1   ƒx A1

Cell H5 is in column H, row 5

Take note

In practice, worksheet size is limited not by the number of cells available but by the amount of free computer memory.

Take note

An Excel file can contain several worksheets, which together form a workbook (see page 78).

Options

- Click on the scroll bar arrows to move the display one row or column at a time.

- Click on the grey scroll areas to move by one screenful.

- Drag the buttons on the scroll bars to move by large amounts.

- Click on a cell to make it active.

- Press the keyboard's arrow keys to make an adjacent cell active.

- Select **Edit > Go To** (or press [**Ctrl**]+[**G**] or [**F5**]). Enter a new cell reference and click on **OK** to make any cell on the sheet active.

Moving around

The main difficulty with any spreadsheet program is that you can only ever see a small proportion of the worksheet at any one time. However, there are scroll bars to the right and below the grid, which allow you to move around the worksheet and see other areas of the sheet.

One cell is always **active**. This is the cell where data can be entered (initially A1). The active cell is identified by a thicker border; the letter at the top of the column and the row number on the left are highlighted in blue. Any cell can be made the active cell by clicking on it; using the scroll bars or arrow keys to move around; or selecting a new cell with the **Edit > Go To** menu option. Only one cell can be active at a time.

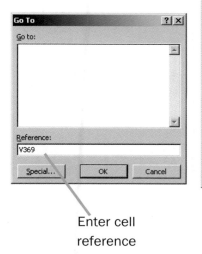

Enter cell reference

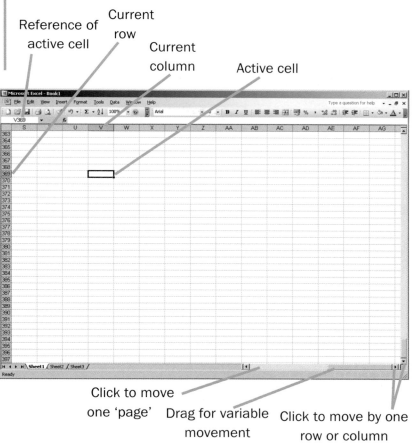

Reference of active cell

Current row

Current column

Active cell

Click to move one 'page'

Drag for variable movement

Click to move by one row or column

Saving the worksheet

It is essential to get into the habit of saving your work regularly. The data you have entered so far exists only in the computer's memory and it will be lost unless you save it in a file before leaving Excel.

The worksheet data may also be lost if the program – or Windows – crashes (i.e. produces a fatal error message that results in the application being forcibly closed). This does not happen often but when it does, it's usually at the most inconvenient moment! So, save your work frequently.

Although you can undo most actions by pressing **[Ctrl]** + **[Z]**, there are occasions when you can damage a worksheet by some unintended formatting change or the application of an incorrect formula. Always save the sheet before any major change.

1 Click on **File** in the menu bar and then on **Save** in the menu that drops down. A standard Windows file box appears.

2 Double-click on the drive and then on the folder; do not store your files in the Excel program folder; use a new folder for your data. (The **Save As** window has a button for creating a new folder if necessary.)

1 Open **Save As** box

2 Select drive and folder

Click to create new folder

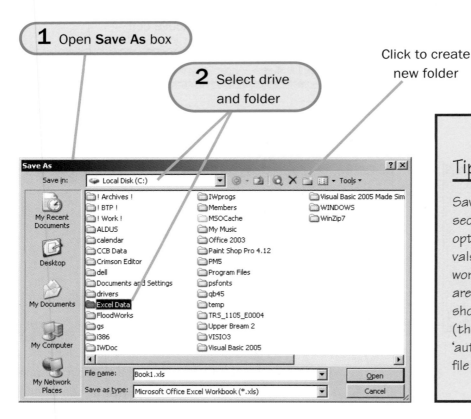

Tip

Saving takes only a few seconds, so use the Save option at regular intervals. Never have more work unsaved than you are prepared to re-create should the worst happen (though Excel saves an 'autorecovery' copy of the file periodically).

3 Type a filename, following the usual Windows rules. Do not enter an extension; Excel automatically adds .XLS for you.

4 Click on **Save**.

The file is saved, the new name appears on the title bar, and you can continue editing.

The next time you choose **File > Save** you will not have to supply a name; the current worksheet will replace the previous version in the file.

You will need to devise some logical naming scheme for your Excel files. Names need to be brief but remind you of what the files contain. Bear in mind that you may want to create several different versions of the same file, so allow for the inclusion of some further identification (e.g. 'Sales 2006 North Actual', 'Sales 2007 West Projected').

Take note

When you save a file, the changes you have made become permanent. You cannot use Undo to roll back any changes made before the save.

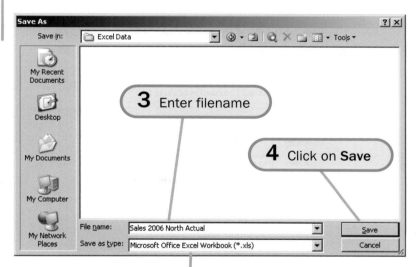

3 Enter filename

4 Click on **Save**

Change type if you want to use the data in a different application; select the **Template** option if you want to use this file as the basis for other files

Toolbar shortcuts for File menu

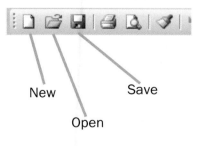

New

Open

Save

Tip

If you need to keep copies of previous versions of a file, do so by storing them in different folders. For instance, if you update files monthly, create folders that have the month and year in the folder name.

You can add other information relating to the file using the **File > Properties** option. Enter any relevant details and click on **OK**. Resave the file with **File > Save**.

Enter file details on
Summary tab

Sales 2006 North Actual.xls Properties   ❌

| General | Summary | Statistics | Contents | Custom |

Title: Sales 2006 North - Actual

Subject: Sales data for Northern region (2006)

Author: Stephen Morris

Manager:

Company: Butford Technical Publishing Ltd

Category:

Keywords:

Comments: Figures for latest month may be incomplete

Hyperlink base:

Template:

☐ Save preview picture

         OK   Cancel

Click on **OK** to
save details

If you want to save a new version of the worksheet, leaving the original intact, choose **Save As** from the **File** menu, instead of **Save**. You are then given the opportunity to enter a new name or choose a new folder. The original file will remain as it was when it was last saved. This gives you a simple way to use an existing file as the basis for a new one.

Tip

To resave quickly, just press [Ctrl]+[S] or click on the Save button on the toolbar. The current worksheet replaces the last saved version.

Take note

If you attempt to leave Excel without saving the changes you have made, the program will prompt you to do so. You are presented with three options.

Click on Yes to save the changes, No to abandon them or Cancel to continue working on the file without saving it.

Tip

if you save Summary information, remember to keep it up to date.

Load options

There are four ways to load an Excel worksheet:

- Select **Open** from the **File** menu; choose the drive, folder and file from the file-list box.

- Click on the **Open** button on the toolbar as a shortcut to the **File > Open** option.

- Click on one of the most recently used files, listed at the bottom of the menu.

- Select an option in the task pane.

Loading a worksheet

Providing you have saved your worksheet, it can be easily loaded again the next time you start up Excel.

The **File** menu contains an option to load a worksheet (**Open**) and lists recently-used files. There is also a **New** option, which should be used if you want to start again from scratch. The options are all duplicated in the task pane.

There is no need to reload the worksheet if Excel has been temporarily suspended: just click on any visible part of the Excel window or, if it has been minimized, click on the Excel button at the bottom of the Desktop. Alternatively, select Excel using **[Alt]+[Tab]** or **[Alt]+[Esc]**.

Select file in the Open dialog box

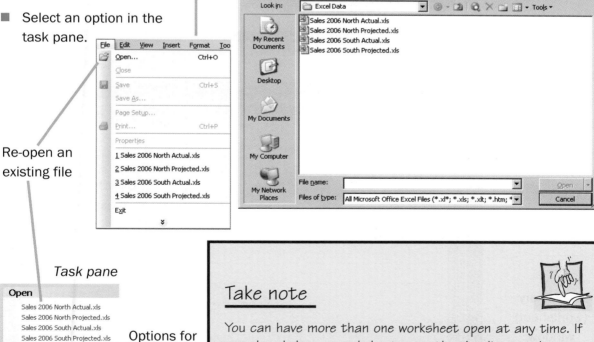

Re-open an existing file

Task pane

Options for new files

Take note

You can have more than one worksheet open at any time. If you already have a worksheet open, then loading another one does not close the first one. For details of how to handle several worksheets at once, see Chapter 6.

The worksheet window

The Excel display considered so far has actually consisted of two windows: the main Excel window and a subsidiary window containing the worksheet file. Initially, the subsidiary window is maximized, so it completely fills the parent window (the Excel window).

If you click on the lower of the two **Maximize** buttons, the second window will be reduced in size and the distinction between the two will become more apparent. This is a useful option when you need to see two sheets at once. At other times, you will have a greater workspace if you maximize the worksheet window.

Hide the task pane by clicking on its **Close** button; redisplay the pane with **View > Task Pane**.

Tip

Unless it is essential that you see other windows while working on a sheet, keep the Excel window maximized. Otherwise, the screen can become very confusing.

Click here to reduce Excel window size

Control menu for Excel

Control menu for worksheet window

Use **Window** menu to switch between open worksheets

Main Excel window (parent window)

Click here to reduce worksheet window size

Click here to maximize

Subsidiary (worksheet) window

Microsoft Excel

File Edit View Insert Format Tools Data Window Help

100%   Arial   10   B I U   %

A1   fx

Sales 2006 North Actual.xls

	A	B	C	D	E	F	G	H	I	J
1										
2										
3			TOTAL SALES NORTH							
4										
5			2006	2005						
6		1st Qtr	1092	1048						
7		2nd Qtr	718	623						
8		3rd Qtr	1953	1955						
9		4th Qtr	908	705						
10										
11		TOTAL	6677	6336						
12										
13										
14										
15										
16										
17										
18										
19										
20										
21										
22										
23										
24										
25										
26										

Sheet1 Sheet2 Sheet3

Getting Help

Help options

- The **Help** menu leads to either the **Office Assistant** or the **Assistance** box, and has links to the Internet Help options. You can also activate Excel and re-install damaged or missing program files.

- The **Office Assistant** lets you type in direct questions and then lists Help topics that match your text, in a similar way to the **Assistance** box. The **Office Assistant** is turned on or off using an option in the **Help** menu.

- **Labels** are displayed under the toolbar buttons if you rest the pointer over them.

- The **status bar** gives instructions when you select a menu option.

To get Help at any time, select **Help > Microsoft Excel Help**. An **Assistance** box is added to the task pane. Type a query into the box and the pane will display topics that may be relevant. Click on one of these topics to get Help. The Help topic is displayed in a separate window.

In the task pane, the buttons at the top let you navigate through the Help you've previously selected.

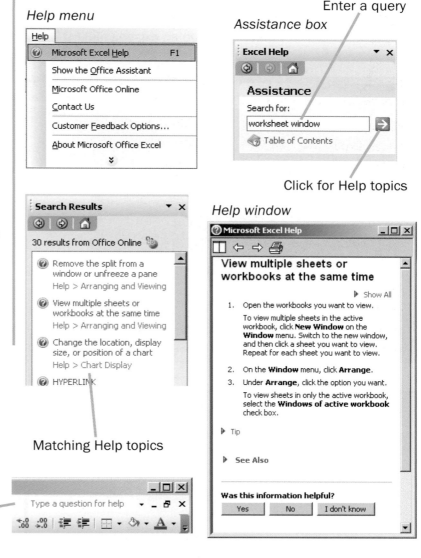

Help menu

Assistance box

Enter a query

Click for Help topics

Search Results

Matching Help topics

Help window

Reminder label

Another place to type a query

Closing a file

You can close a worksheet window without leaving Excel. If you have another worksheet open, this will be displayed, Closing the last worksheet gives you a completely empty Excel window, into which you can load a new worksheet.

When all window have been closed, most options in the drop-down menus will be greyed out, indicating that they are unavailable.

Options for starting a new file (an empty file or one based on an existing file)

Close options

There are several ways to close the worksheet file:

■ Select **Close** from the **File menu**.

■ Click on the subsidiary window's control menu and then on **Close**.

■ Press [**Ctrl**]+[**W**].

■ Click on the subsidiary window's **Close** button.

Options for starting a new file based on a template

Tip

To start a new file, select File > New and then choose from the options in the task pane. You can start with the default worksheet, an existing folder or one of the supplied templates.

Alternatively, click on the New button on the toolbar. A blank worksheet is loaded (identical to the default worksheet).

Take note

You can save a worksheet as a template (with an XLT extension) rather than a normal XLS style. The template can be used as the basis for future worksheets.

Closing Excel

Exit options

- Click on the **Close** button, choose **Close** from the control menu or press **[Alt]+[F4]** to end the program.

- Alternatively, select **Exit** from the **File** menu (or **[Alt] [F] [X]**) to close Excel.

- Click on the **Minimize** button to reduce Excel to an icon; the program and worksheet stay in memory.

- Click on another window to push Excel to the back without closing it down.

- **[Alt]+[Tab]** and **[Alt]+[Esc]** provide alternative methods of selecting other applications without closing Excel.

You can get out of Excel – either permanently or temporarily – using any of the usual Windows methods.

◆ If you close Excel down, then you will have to reload your worksheet at the start of the next session (or begin a new worksheet). Loading is described on **page 9**.

◆ If you temporarily move to some other Windows application, the current worksheet will be maintained in memory (but do save it first, just in case – see **page 6**).

Click here ...

... then here

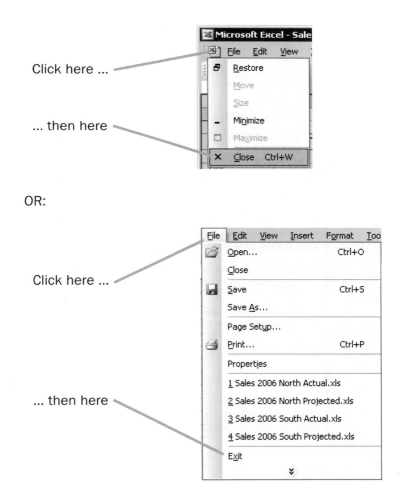

OR:

Click here ...

... then here

Take note

When you close Excel, you are prompted to save any open worksheets that have not been saved since changes were made (see page 6).

Exercises

1 Open Excel, displaying a blank worksheet, and switch off the task pane.

2 Move the cursor to cell B3, type the text 'Total Sales North' and press **[Enter]**.

3 Use the **Go To** option to move to cell Z500 and then back to cell A1.

4 Save the worksheet as 'Total Sales.xls'.

5 Save the worksheet as a text file and view it in Notepad.

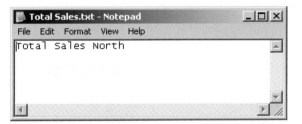

6 Re-open 'Total Sales.xls' and arrange the windows so that you can see both Notepad and Excel versions.

7 Add summary information to the XLS file and resave it.

8 Search for Help on displaying multiple worksheets.

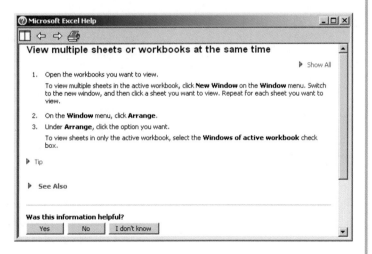

9 Close each of the worksheets and then close Excel.

2 Working with cells

Entering data

Excel always starts with a blank worksheet. Entering data is simply a matter of selecting a cell and then typing a value. You can enter numbers or text in any cell. As an example, create a worksheet with the simple table below.

1 Click on cell B2 so that it is the active cell.

2 Type 'TOTAL SALES: NORTH'. As you do so, the text appears in the cell and, simultaneously, in the formula bar, above the column labels.

3 Press [**Enter**] when the text is complete. The cursor moves down to the next cell (in this case, B3).

4 Now click on C4 to enter '2006', and D4 for '2005'.

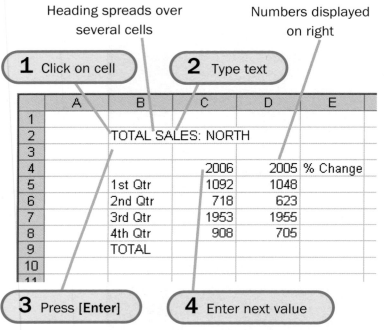

Heading spreads over several cells

Numbers displayed on right

1 Click on cell

2 Type text

3 Press [**Enter**]

4 Enter next value

Don't worry about the appearance of the text to start with. It will look messy when you enter it but you can tidy it up later by adding colour, changing column widths and so on.

Take note

The main block of eight numbers are placed on the right of the cells. Excel recognises most of the other entries as text and places them on the left of the cell. However, it treats the years 2006 and 2005 as numbers, putting them on the right of the cells. These values will be changed to text later (see page 18).

Tip

You can also complete an entry by pressing one of the cursor keys or clicking on another cell.

If you want to move left or right within the entry you are making, you need to switch to the formula bar (see page 20).

5 Enter '% Change' in E4.

6 Enter the row titles in cells B5 to B9. (Here, you do not need to click on the cells below B5 because the cursor moves down when you press [**Enter**].)

7 Click on C5 and enter the value '1092'.

8 Fill in the other seven values in the cells from C6 to C8 and D5 to D8.

The totals will be calculated by Excel when a formula is entered (see **page 30**).

(see **page 30**)

Tip

If you start making an entry in the wrong cell, press [Esc] and no change will be made. Anything you have typed will disappear and the original cell contents (if any) will be restored.

Excel always tries to decide what sort of data is being entered:

◆ If the value starts with a number, + or – sign, and contains only numeric characters, it is treated as a numeric value.

◆ If the entry begins with a + or – sign (and also contains letters) or an = sign, Excel assumes it is a formula.

◆ If the entry looks like a date or time (e.g. 4/6/06, 4-6 or 3:30), Excel converts it to a standard date/time format.

◆ In all other cases, Excel assumes the entry is a piece of text.

Numeric values and the results of numeric formulae are always aligned on the right-hand side of the columns. Dates and times are also right-aligned. By default, text entries are placed on the left.

Formula bar

Microsoft Excel - Sales 2006 North Actual.xls

File Edit View Insert Format Tools Data Window Help

100% Arial

D8   *fx* 705

	A	B	C	D	E	F	G
1							
2		TOTAL SALES: NORTH					
3							

Autofill lets you create sets of values quickly. To repeat the same value over a number of cells, enter the value and then drag the small square in the bottom right-hand corner of the cell over the required range. To create a sequence of values, enter the first two values, select the two cells and then drag the small square over the new range.

Autofill

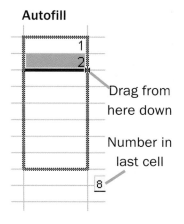

Drag from here down

Number in last cell

17

Display formats

If you want a numeric value to be treated as text, start by typing an apostrophe ('). This has a special meaning for Excel and indicates that the cell contains a text value; the apostrophe will not be displayed in the cell.

Excel assumes that a non-numeric entry is text, so you only need an apostrophe where there might otherwise be confusion:

◆ When the entry looks like a number, date or time

◆ When the entry starts with =, + or – but is not a formula

◆ When you want a real apostrophe to be displayed at the start of the label (start by typing two apostrophes).

Basic steps

■ **To change the 2006 and 2005 labels to text:**

1 Click on C4.

2 Type '2006 and press [**Enter**].

3 Click on D4.

4 Type '2005 and press [**Enter**].

The labels are now shown on the left of the cell.

Take note

When you change a number to text, Excel puts a green triangle in the top left-hand corner of the cell. When you click on the cell, a warning symbol is shown to the left. Put the pointer on this symbol to see a pop-up message that tells you how the cell has been formatted; click on the warning symbol for a menu of options.

Tip

It is often easier to retype an entry than to edit an existing entry. See page 20 for editing options.

Tip

Text that is too wide to fit in a cell is displayed in adjacent empty cells.

You can also centre a title in a row so that it stretches over several columns – see page 67.

Click for menu

Put pointer on box to show warning message

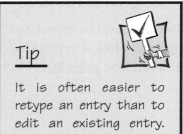

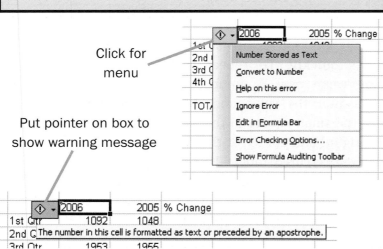

Numbers

For the **General** format, the type of display depends on the numeric value:

- Whole numbers (integers) are displayed with no decimal point (e.g. 123).

- Decimals are shown with as many decimal places as are needed, and with a zero to the left of the decimal point for numbers less than 1 (e.g. 12.3, 1.23, 0.123, 0.0123).

- Very large and very small numbers are converted to the **Scientific** (or **Exponential**) format (e.g. 1.23E+09) – see the Excel Help for details.

- Anything that looks like a date or time is converted to the most appropriate **Date** or **Time** format.

- If the cell is too narrow to show a number, it expands to fit. However, if you have already changed the width, the cell is filled with # marks (though the number is still held safely in memory).

Numbers are displayed using the **General** format, unless you specify otherwise. With this format, Excel selects the most appropriate style in each individual case, using the least number of decimal places possible (and none at all for whole numbers).

In many cases this leads to an untidy display and you will want to change the format; details of how to do this are given in **Chapter 5**.

Column width changed; too narrow to display numbers

	A	B	C	D	E	F	G
1							
2							
3							
4		Integers	Decimals	Exponential		Narrow	
5						column	
6							
7		1	1.2	6.00E+19		###	
8		23	4.867	2.30E+11		###	
9		235	2.97612	3.40E+27		###	
10		0	0.23	4.00E-10		###	
11		-1	0.00004	6.23E-14		###	
12						751717	
13							

Place pointer over cell to see value in pop-up label

Take note

You can apply different formats to individual cells or groups of cells. For instance, you can put a currency symbol in front of money amounts or separate thousands with commas – see Chapter 5.

You can also design your own format – search for 'custom format' in the Excel Help for full instructions on setting up your own customised format.

Simple editing

If you make a mistake, it's easily put right; there's no need to start all over again. The contents of any cell can be replaced or revised with very little effort.

Displayed value
temporarily truncated
during editing

Formula
bar

Editing
cursor

	B2	▼ ✕ ✓ ƒₓ	TOTAL SALES: NORTH				
	A	B	C	D	E	F	G
1							
2		TOTAL SA					
3							
4			2006	2005	% Change		
5		1st Qtr	1092	1048			
6		2nd Qtr	718	623			
7		3rd Qtr	1953	1955			
8		4th Qtr	908	705			
9		TOTAL					
10							
11							

Basic steps

- **To edit the contents of a cell:**

1 Click on the cell that contains the incorrect value. The value or formula appears in the formula bar.

2 To replace the value altogether, just type a new entry; there's no need to delete the existing value.

3 To change the value, click on the formula bar. Use the cursor keys or mouse to position the cursor within the value, then use **[Delete]** to erase the character to the right of the cursor or **[Backspace]** to delete to the left. Insert characters by typing at the cursor position.

Take note

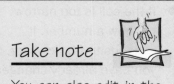

You can also edit in the cell by double-clicking on it – the effect is the same. Any changes you make in the cell are duplicated in the formual bar.

Basic steps

- **To delete the contents of a cell:**

1 Click on the cell.

2 Press [**Delete**]. (This is a shortcut for the **Edit > Clear > All** command.)

<u>Tip</u>

You can delete the contents of several cells by highlighting a range (see <u>page 22</u>) and then pressing [Delete].

If you realise a mistake is being made as you are entering data, you can press [**Esc**] to abandon the entry. Whatever was in the cell beforehand is unaffected.

However, if a wrong entry has been made, or the contents of a cell are no longer needed, the entry can be deleted.

Mistakes can usually be cancelled, even after completing an entry, by pressing [**Ctrl**]+[**Z**]. This **Undo** action restores the original contents of the last cell changed and can be used after editing, replacing or deleting the contents of a cell. Each time you press [**Ctrl**]+[**Z**], another action is cancelled.

Similarly, the **Redo** option repeats actions that have been cancelled by **Undo**. The **Redo** option is included in the **Edit** menu below **Undo**; alternatively, press [**Ctrl**]+[**Y**].

You can undo several actions at once by clicking on the **Undo** drop-down button on the toolbar. The list shows the most recent actions and any that you highlight are cancelled. Click on an entry to delete that action and all those above; click outside the list to leave the worksheet unchanged.

In a similar way, if you add the **Redo** button to the toolbar, this has a drop-down list of items that have been cancelled by **Undo**.

<u>Take note</u>

Do not press the space bar and [Enter] to blank out a cell as this can cause problems in formulae that refer to the cell.

This will also stop text spreading across from neighbouring cells.

Undo last action

Most recent actions to be undone; highlight and click

Undo list

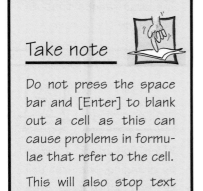

<u>Take note</u>

Excel does not store everything you do; sometimes you will not be able to undo actions, so make sure you save regularly (see <u>page 6</u>). Get into the habit of pressing [Ctrl]+[S] every few minutes.

Ranges

Many operations within Excel require you to mark out ranges of cells. For example, you may want to add together all the numbers in a range of cells; you will also want to change the display format for ranges of cells (see **Chapter 7**).

A range is a group of cells that forms a rectangle. The range is identified by the cells in the top left-hand and bottom right-hand corners of the rectangle, separated by a colon. For instance, the range reference A1:B3 identifies a range containing six cells: A1, A2, A3, B1, B2 and B3.

A range can be anything from a single cell to the entire worksheet.

Basic steps

- **To mark a range on the worksheet:**

1 Move the pointer to the cell in the top left-hand corner of the range.

2 Press and hold the mouse button, then drag the pointer to the cell at the bottom right-hand corner of the range.

3 Release the mouse button; the range is highlighted.

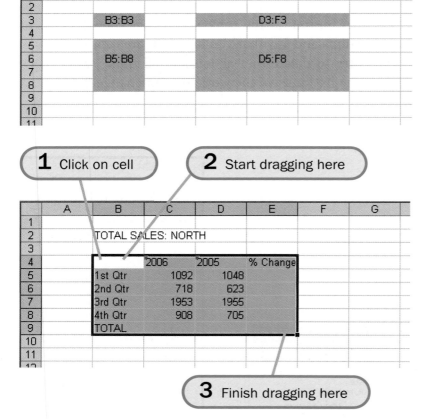

Tip

As an alternative to dragging the pointer, click on the first cell, press and hold [Shift], then click on the last cell. This is particularly useful for large ranges that do not fit on the screen.

Take note

When you mark a range by dragging, the first cell is not highlighted, even though it is included in the range.

Selecting

- To mark a single cell just click on it.
- To mark a whole row or column, click on the row number or column letter.
- To mark the entire worksheet, click on the square in the top left-hand corner of the worksheet.

You can highlight whole rows or columns, or the entire sheet by clicking on the worksheet borders.

You can select more than one range at a time by holding down **[Ctrl]** while you mark the blocks, rows or columns (see illustration below).

If you click anywhere else after you have marked a block, the block marking disappears.

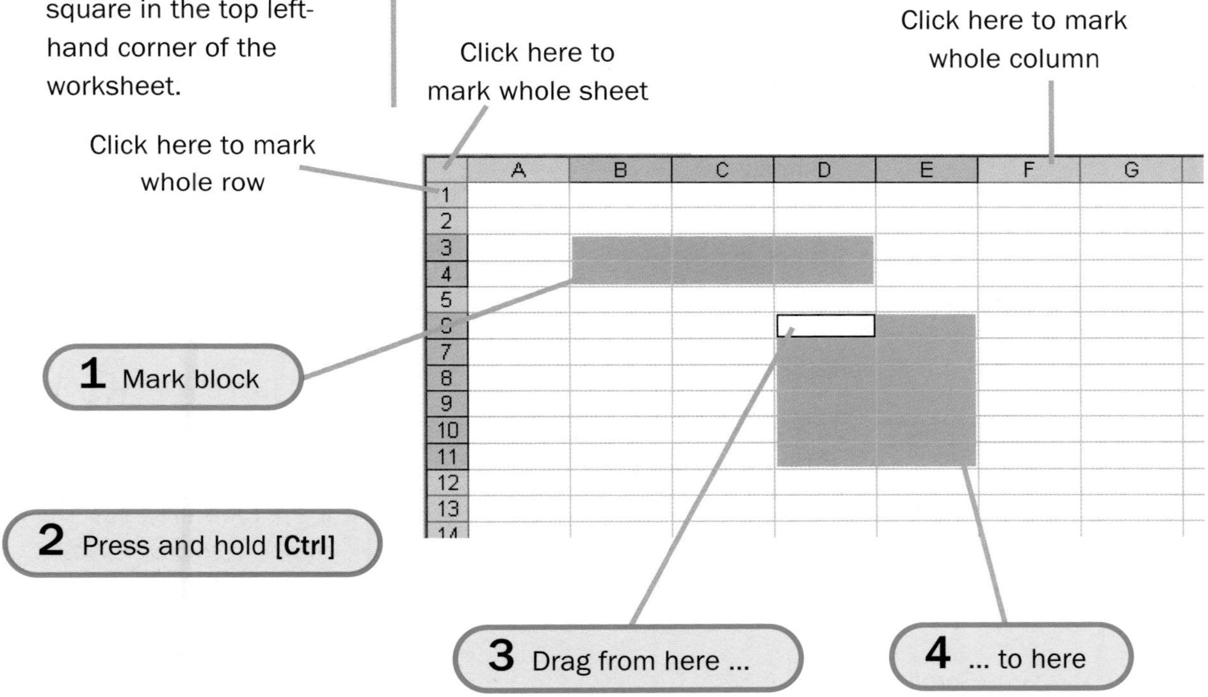

Click here to mark whole column
Click here to mark whole sheet
Click here to mark whole row
1 Mark block
2 Press and hold [Ctrl]
3 Drag from here ...
4 ... to here

Tip

You can change the area of the worksheet that is visible by selecting a different zoom percentage from the box on the toolbar. You can also type in a specific percentage or click on Selection to zoom in on the current selected range.

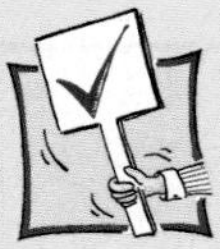

Type new zoom value
100%
200%
100%
75%
50%
25%
Selection
Select zoom value

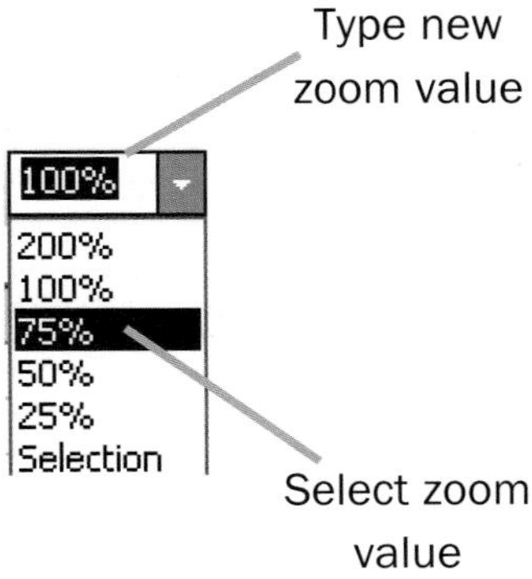

Freezing titles

On large worksheets, you may need to be able to see the titles at the top of the sheet, or the row headings on the left, when you are working with data at some distant point. You can do this by **freezing** the titles.

The **Window > Freeze Panes** option allows you to fix the rows above the current cell so that they will no longer scroll out of view. However, if you move the cursor to the right, the rows will still scroll right. Similarly, the columns to the left of the current cell are fixed and will only scroll up and down.

To free the titles again, select **Window > Unfreeze Panes**.

Basic steps

1 Click on the cell in the top-left corner of the area that is to move freely (cell C5 in the example).

2 Select **Window > Freeze Panes**.

You can move anywhere on the sheet (including the title areas) but the titles are always visible. In the example, columns A and B are fixed, as are rows 1 to 4.

After freezing, completely fixed

Scrolls horizontally

	A	B	E	F	G	H	I
				Order Summary			
4	No.		Company	Reference	Qty	Unit Price	
38	38		Southbury Supplies	KB-995/02	23	2.87	
39	39		Southbury Supplies	FB-230/03	401	0.45	
40	40		ABT Ltd	KB-995/02	8	2.87	
41	41		Westwood Enterprises	RT9-405-356	12	12.45	
42	42		Southbury Supplies	KB-995/02	54	2.87	
43	43		Southbury Supplies	SB-087/00	340	80.03	
44	44		ABT Ltd	AFT88/2/W/a	7	17.95	

E38 — *fx* Southbury Supplies

Scrolls normally

Scrolls vertically

Tip

To fix rows only, put the cursor in column A; to fix columns only, put the cursor in row 1.

Take note

The Window > Split command divides the sheet into two or four areas, in a similar way to the Freeze Panes option, but any of these can be scrolled independently of the others.

Basic steps

- **To create a new toolbar:**

1 Select **View > Toolbars**.

2 Click on **Customize**.

3 Click on the **Toolbars** tab.

4 Click on the **New** button. Enter a name for the toolbar and click on **OK**.

5 Click on the **Commands** tab.

6 Select a **Category**.

7 Drag an icon from the **Commands** list to the new toolbar (which will be 'floating' somewhere nearby).

Repeat steps 6 and 7 until the toolbar is complete, then click on **Close**.

Custom toolbar

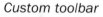

Excel is equipped with a number of toolbars, which can be customised to suit your own preferences. The **View > Toolbars** option lists them. Clicking on the boxes next to the toolbar names displays or hides them.

To change the contents of the toolbars, click on **Customize**:

◆ New buttons are added to the toolbars by dragging the buttons from the **Commands** tab of the dialog box to the toolbars.

◆ Buttons are removed from toolbars by dragging them off.

◆ Clicking on the **New** button creates a new toolbar.

Defaults ———
Available toolbars

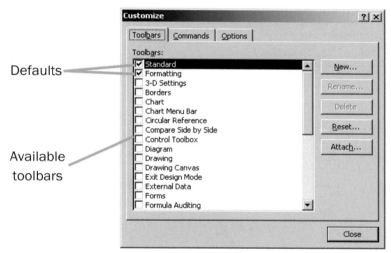

Take note

Toolbars are added as 'floating' windows but if you drag them into the toolbar area at the top of the screen, they lose their Close buttons and titles. Similarly, dragging any toolbar (including the default toolbars) into the centre of the screen converts it into a floating toolbar.

Click to show other buttons or change the contents of the toolbar

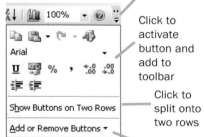

Click to activate button and add to toolbar

Click to split onto two rows

Click to list available buttons or change the contents of the toolbar

25

Comments

Data can be annotated by attaching a comment to any cell. The comment takes the form of a piece of text entered into a dialog box using **Insert > Comment**. All the usual editing facilities are available. Comments are saved with the worksheet.

The comment attached to a cell is displayed if you pause with the pointer over the cell. Selecting **View > Comments** displays the **Comments** toolbar, which provides viewing and editing facilities. All comments for the worksheet can be viewed and any comment can be edited or deleted.

Basic steps

1 Click on a cell.

2 Select **Insert > Comment**.

3 Type the text into the comment box.

4 Click on a different cell.

A red triangle in the top right-hand corner of the cell indicates that a comment is attached.

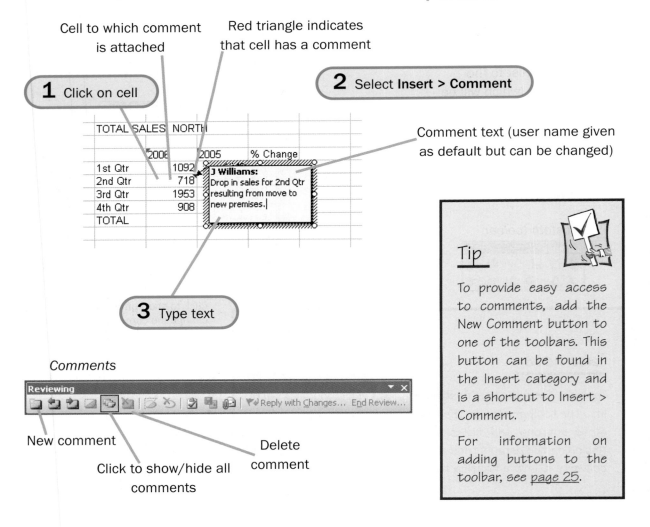

Cell to which comment is attached

Red triangle indicates that cell has a comment

1 Click on cell

2 Select **Insert > Comment**

TOTAL SALES NORTH

	2006	2005	% Change
1st Qtr	1092		
2nd Qtr	718		
3rd Qtr	1953		
4th Qtr	908		
TOTAL			

J Williams:
Drop in sales for 2nd Qtr resulting from move to new premises.

Comment text (user name given as default but can be changed)

3 Type text

Comments

Reviewing

New comment

Click to show/hide all comments

Delete comment

Tip

To provide easy access to comments, add the New Comment button to one of the toolbars. This button can be found in the Insert category and is a shortcut to Insert > Comment.

For information on adding buttons to the toolbar, see page 25.

Options tabs

- The **View** tab determines which elements of the worksheet are displayed (for example, whether grid lines are displayed).

- The **Edit** tab changes the editing options (for example, the cell that is selected after pressing [**Enter**]).

- The **General** tab determines settings such as the number of previously-opened files listed in the File menu, the default font, the default location for worksheet files and the user name.

- The **Color** tab lets you change the default colours.

- The **Save** tab specifies the frequency with which Excel saves an autorecovery copy of the worksheet.

User options

You can change a large number of options that determine the way in which Excel is used. Select **Tools** > **Options** to display the **Options** dialog box. This includes a number of tabs for different categories of options.

To change the options, click on a tab, make the changes and click on **OK**.

View tab

Display or hide grid lines

General tab

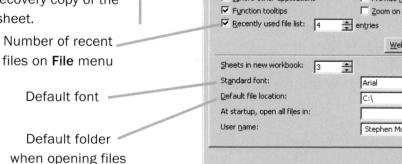

Number of recent files on **File** menu

Default font

Default folder when opening files

Exercises

1 Start a new worksheet and enter the data as shown below in the range A1:I7. The entry in cell I1 should be entered as a text value. (The main data will be filled in later.) Save the file as Timesheet.xls.

	A	B	C	D	E	F	G	H	I	J
1	Monthly Timesheet								2006	
2										
3	Name:									
4	Month:									
5										
6			Hours					Expenses		
7	Date		Project 1	Project 2	Project 3	Project 4	TOTAL	Details	Amount	
8		1								
9		2								

2 Use the Autofill method to fill in the values 1 to 31 in the range B8:B38.

3 Enter the text shown in the range A39:F45.

37		30								
38		31								
39	Total									
40										
41				SUMMARY		Hours				
42						x Rate				
43						Pay				
44						Expenses				
45						Total Due				
46										

4 Freeze the titles, so that rows 1 to 7 and columns A and B are visible at all times. Resave the file.

5 Add the **New Comment** button to the **Standard** toolbar.

6 Increase the number of recently-used files shown on the **File** menu to 6.

3 Using formulae

Entering a formula

A **formula** is used to calculate the value of a cell from the contents of other cells. For instance, formulae may be used to calculate totals or averages, produce percentages or find the minimum and maximum values in ranges.

A formula consists of a mathematical or text **expression**, which refers to other cells or to constant values. The components ('arguments') of the formula are linked together by **operators** (+, – etc.) You can make formulae more readable by putting spaces on either side of the operators. Formulae must start with an =, + or – sign.

Formula bar

SUM	▼	✕ ✓ ƒ✗	=c5+c6+c7+c8	
	A	B	C	D	E
1					
2		TOTAL SALES: NORTH			
3					
4			2006	2005	% Change
5		1st Qtr	1092	1048	
6		2nd Qtr	718	623	
7		3rd Qtr	1953	1955	
8		4th Qtr	908	705	
9		TOTAL	=c5+c6+c7+c8		
10					

Formula being entered

Current cell

C9	▼		ƒ✗	=C5+C6+C7+C8	
	A	B	C	D	E
1					
2		TOTAL SALES: NORTH			
3					
4			2006	2005	% Change
5		1st Qtr	1092	1048	
6		2nd Qtr	718	623	
7		3rd Qtr	1953	1955	
8		4th Qtr	908	705	
9		TOTAL	4671		
10					

Formula

Result of formula

Basic steps

■ **To enter a formula:**

1 Click on the cell where you want to show the result (e.g. C9).

2 Type the formula. For example:

=c5+c6+c7+c8

(You can use either upper or lower case letters.) The formula appears simultaneously in the cell and the formula bar.

3 Press [**Enter**]. The result of the calculation is shown in the cell.

When you click on this cell again, the formula is shown in the formula bar, where it can be edited. When you click on the formula bar or double-click on the cell, cell references in the formula are shown in different colours, and the cells concerned are highlighted by boxes in the same colours.

Take note

There is an easier way of doing this type of calculation, using the SUM function – see <u>page 36</u>.

Tip

Instead of typing a cell reference, click on the cell you want.

■ To edit a formula:

1 Click on the cell containing the formula.

2 Click on the formula in the formula bar.

3 With the usual cursor and editing keys, make the corrections.

4 Press **[Enter]**. The new result is displayed.

To handle an error:

1 Click on the cell.

2 Click on the warning symbol.

3 Select the appropriate option from the pop-up menu.

If you make a mistake and a numeric formula cannot be calculated (for instance, you divide by zero or refer to a text cell), Excel displays #VALUE! in the cell and puts a green triangle in the top left-hand corner of the cell. When you click on the cell, a warning symbol is shown; clicking on that gives a pop-up menu of options.

Other errors may be harder to identify and will not produce an error message. For instance, typing a – (minus) sign instead of + (plus) gives a valid answer but produces the wrong value.

Error

	C9	▼	_fx_ =C5+C6+C7+B8		
	A	B	C	D	E
1					
2		TOTAL SALES: NORTH			
3					
4			2006	2005	% Change
5		1st Qtr	1092	1048	
6		2nd Qtr	718	623	
7		3rd Qtr	1953	1955	
8		4th Qtr	908	705	
9		TOTA ◇ ▼	#VALUE!		
10					
11			Error in Value		
12			Help on this error		
13					
14			Show Calculation Steps...		
15			Ignore Error		
16			Edit in Formula Bar		
17					
18			Error Checking Options...		
19			Show Formula Auditing Toolbar		
20					
21					

Error indicator

Error options

Operators

Five main arithmetic operators are used to determine how values are combined. A formula consists of an alternating sequence of values and operators, usually starting and ending with a value (the only exceptions are the use of a minus sign to negate a value and the percentage symbol).

The calculation is not carried out from left to right but according to the following rules:

◆　Negation and percentages are done first.

◆　Raising to the power (∧) is calculated next (also called **exponentiation**).

◆　After that come any multiplications and divisions (* /).

◆　Finally, additions and subtractions (+ –) are performed.

For example:

> **= B4 + B5 * 2**

Here, the contents of cell B5 are multiplied by 2 before being added to the contents of B4.

For text calculations, only the & operator is allowed. This adds one piece of text to the end of another. For example:

> **= "Mon" & "day"**

This formula produces the result 'Monday'. You cannot use + to combine text in a formula.

The following numeric operators are recognised:

∧　Raising to the power (e.g. 2^3 is 8)

*　Multiplication

/　Division

+　Addition

–　Subtraction

You can also use:

–　Negation (in front of a number)

%　Percentage (after a number)

For text formulae:

&　Combines strings (concatenation)

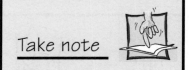

Take note

Plus and minus signs are also used in numbers displayed or entered using the Scientific format — see the Excel Help for details of this.

The division sign (/) also appears in dates and the percentage sign (%) is displayed on cells formatted as percentages.

Take note

Put a minus sign (–) in front of a value to negate it or follow it with a percentage sign (%). For example, 2*–3 gives –6; multiplying by 5% is the same as multiplying by 0.05. Negations and percentages are done before the other operations.

Main points

- Calculations start inside the innermost pair of brackets and work outwards.

- Every opening bracket must have a corresponding closing bracket (Excel highlights the matching opening bracket for you every time you type a closing bracket in the formula bar).

- You can nest up to seven pairs of brackets.

Using brackets

You can use **brackets** (parentheses) to change the order of calculation. Anything inside a pair of brackets is calculated first.

For example, the percentage change in E5 is calculated by:

$$= (C5 - D5) / D5$$

The brackets are essential here; if there were no brackets the division would be carried out first, giving a result of 1091 (i.e. C5 - 1, since D5 / D5 = 1).

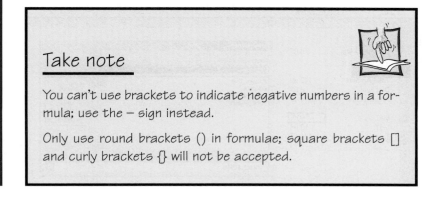

Number of decimal places will be changed later

You can also **nest** brackets: i.e. place one set of brackets inside another. For example:

$$= (100 - (A8 + 1) * 5) + 1$$

If the value in A8 is 7, the result is 61.

Names

Working with ranges can be cumbersome, particularly on large worksheets where a formula may refer to a range that is some distance away. Therefore Excel allows you to attach a name to any cell or range. This name can be used in any formula in place of the cell or range reference.

Names can be up to 255 characters long (far more than you should ever use), consisting of letters, numbers, full stops and the underscore. Other characters are not allowed. The name must start with a letter or underscore and must not include spaces.

Upper and lower case letters are treated the same but the name is stored exactly as you type it, so it is a good idea to mix lower case letters and capitals. When a name is referenced in a formula, Excel converts it to the same mixture of upper and lower case.

Basic steps

- **To add a name:**

1 Mark the cell or range to which the name is to be applied.

2 Select the **Name** option from the **Insert** menu.

3 Click on **Define** in the sub-menu.

4 Type the name and press [**Enter**].

The names you create can be listed in the box above the column letters (where the cell reference is usually shown). Click on the arrow on the right of the box to see the list drop down.

Active cell

Click to jump to named cell

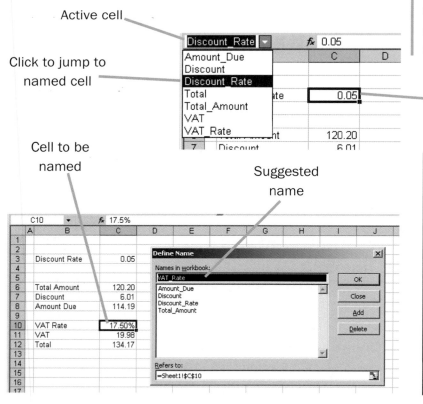

Named cell

Cell to be named

Suggested name

Tip

When entering a new name, Excel usually makes an intelligent guess at the name for you (for instance, it may select an adjacent label, replacing any spaces with underscores).

■ **To use existing labels as names:**

1 Mark a range consisting of the labels and the cells to which they are to be attached.

2 Select **Insert > Name > Create**.

3 Identify the location of the names. For example, **Left Column** means that the names are in a column to the left of the data range.

4 Press [**Enter**] or click on **OK**.

To use a name in a formula, simply substitute the name for the cell reference. In the example in the illustration, the formulae for Discount and Amount Due were originally:

$$= C6 * C3$$

$$= C6 - C7$$

These can be changed to:

$$= Total\_Amount * Discount\_Rate$$

$$= Total\_Amount - Discount$$

Names can either be typed in full or inserted by clicking on the required data cells as you are entering the formula.

Active cell

Click for list of names

Formula using named cells

	A	B	C	D	E
Amount_Due ▼ f_x = Total_Amount - Discount

	A	B	C	D	E
1					
2					
3		Discount Rate	0.05		
4					
5					
6		Total Amount	120.20		
7		Discount	6.01		
8		Amount Due	114.19		
9					

1 Mark range

2 Select **Insert > Name > Create**

Total Amount	120.20
Discount	6.01
Amount Due	114.19

3 Identify names

Create Names ✕

Create names in

☐ Top row
☑ Left column
☐ Bottom row
☐ Right column

OK   Cancel

4 Click on **OK**

Tip

Names are particularly useful where a range is referenced more than once on the worksheet. If you change the definition of the name so that it refers to another range, you will not have to change any of the formulae that use that name.

Excel functions

Excel contains a large number of built-in functions. These are special routines that can be used within a formula to perform particular tasks. For example, the most commonly used function is **SUM**, which calculates the total of all the cells in a specified range.

Other functions include **AVERAGE** to calculate the average of a range; **MIN** and **MAX** to find the smallest and largest numbers in a range; and **INT** to round a value down to the nearest whole number. The **COUNT** function counts the number of cells in a range that contain a value.

The function name is followed by a pair of brackets containing one or more arguments. If there is more than one argument, these are separated by commas. In the case of **SUM**, there need be only one argument: the range to be totalled. You can use either upper or lower case letters for the function and any cell references in the argument.

Functions are used in a formula in the same way as a constant value or cell reference. When the formula is calculated, the function returns a value, which replaces it in the formula.

=SUM(C5:C8)

Function: Argument:
SUM   C5:C8

Take note

The SUM function can take more than one argument. For example, SUM(B6,C9:D12) returns the total of the number in cell B6 plus all the numbers in the range C9:C12.

Using SUM

The **SUM** function can be used in the Total Sales worksheet to replace the rather clumsy formula in C9.

1 Click on C9.

2 Start typing to replace the existing entry:

    =sum(

3 Drag the mouse pointer over the range C5:C8. As you do so the range appears in the formula.

4 Type the closing bracket and press [**Enter**].

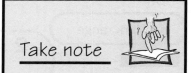

Take note

Other functions are formed in the same way as SUM. For example, AVERAGE(C5:C8) gives the average of the numbers in the range C5:C8 and COUNT(C5:C8) returns the number of cells in the range that contain values.

The average is calculated only from cells that contain values, so AVERAGE( ) is the same as SUM( ) / COUNT( ).

Using AutoSum

■ **To use AutoSum:**

1 Click on the cell where the total is required.

2 Click on the **AutoSum** button. Excel suggests the range to be totalled and marks it with a flashing outline. Check the range very carefully.

3 If the wrong range has been suggested, select a new one by dragging the pointer over it.

4 Press [**Enter**].

The **SUM** function has its own **AutoSum** button on the toolbar. This button lets you apply a **SUM** function with as few as three button clicks. However, it requires some care; it is just as easy to get the sum wrong!

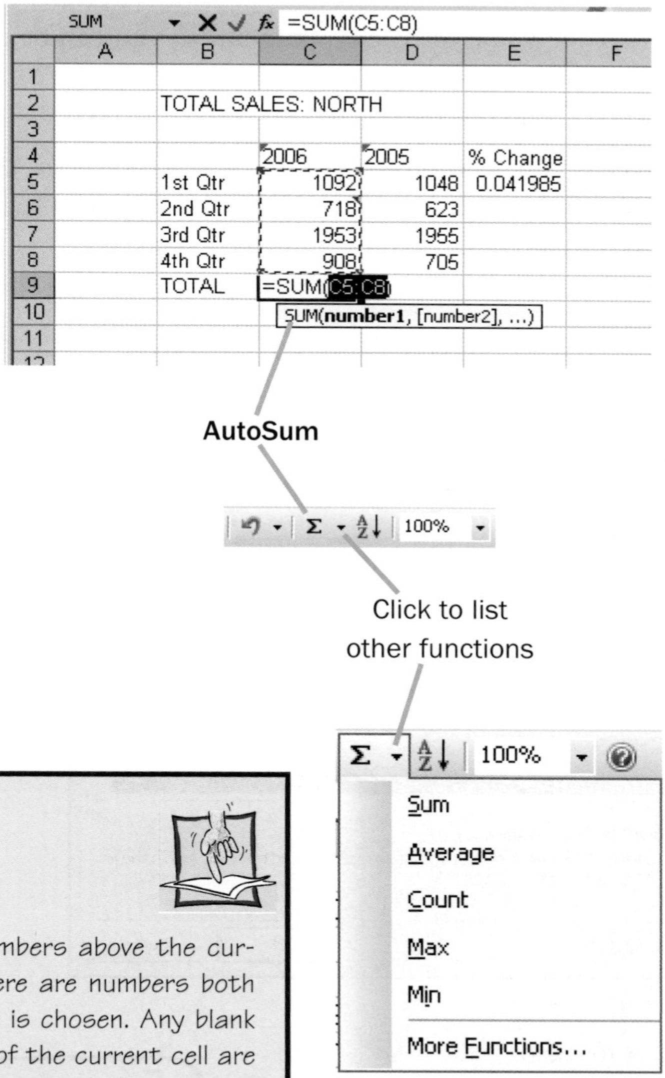

| SUM | ▾ ✕ ✓ *fx* =SUM(C5:C8) |

	A	B	C	D	E	F
1						
2		TOTAL SALES: NORTH				
3						
4			2006	2005	% Change	
5		1st Qtr	1092	1048	0.041985	
6		2nd Qtr	718	623		
7		3rd Qtr	1953	1955		
8		4th Qtr	908	705		
9		TOTAL	=SUM(C5:C8)			
10			SUM(**number1**, [number2], ...)			
11						
12						

AutoSum

| ↻ ▾ | Σ ▾ | ᴬ↓�zᴬ | 100% ▾ |

Click to list other functions

| Σ ▾ | ᴬ↓ᴢᴬ | 100% ▾ | ⓘ |

Sum
Average
Count
Max
Min
More Functions...

Tip

Marking a range by dragging gives you a better chance of getting it right than if you type in the range reference directly.

Take note

AutoSum suggests the column of numbers above the current cell or the row to the left. If there are numbers both above and to the left, the block above is chosen. Any blank cells immediately above or to the left of the current cell are included in the block but if there are gaps in the numbers above or to the left, only those up to the gap are marked.

Inserting a function

There are many different functions in Excel and by far the easiest way of using them is through the **Insert Function** (**fx**) button. This provides a dialog box in which the functions are listed. When you click on a function, its purpose is shown at the bottom of the box.

The **Insert Function** button also provides a dialog box for entering the value for each argument, so you can be certain that you are supplying the correct number of arguments and that they are in the right order.

Each entry can be a constant value, or an expression. You can even nest another function by entering it as part of the value. Functions can be nested up to seven levels.

Basic steps

1 Type the formula up to the point where you need a function.

2 Click on the **Insert Function** button, marked with **fx**, to the left of the formula bar.

3 Select the function category to reduce the list size. (Click on the **All** category if you don't know which set includes the required function.)

4 Click on the required function name.

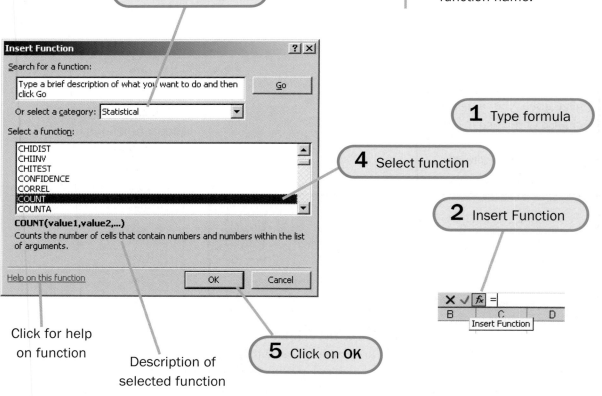

3 Select category

Insert Function

Search for a function:

Type a brief description of what you want to do and then click Go

Go

Or select a category: Statistical

Select a function:

CHIDIST
CHIINV
CHITEST
CONFIDENCE
CORREL
COUNT
COUNTA

4 Select function

COUNT(value1,value2,...)
Counts the number of cells that contain numbers and numbers within the list of arguments.

Help on this function   OK   Cancel

1 Type formula

2 Insert Function

X ✓ fx =
B   C   D
Insert Function

Click for help on function

Description of selected function

5 Click on **OK**

38

5 Click on **OK** to bring up the next dialog box.

6 Add the arguments by entering them directly, clicking on cells or marking ranges.

7 Click on **OK** and the function will be added to the formula.

8 Click on the formula bar to add more elements to the formula.

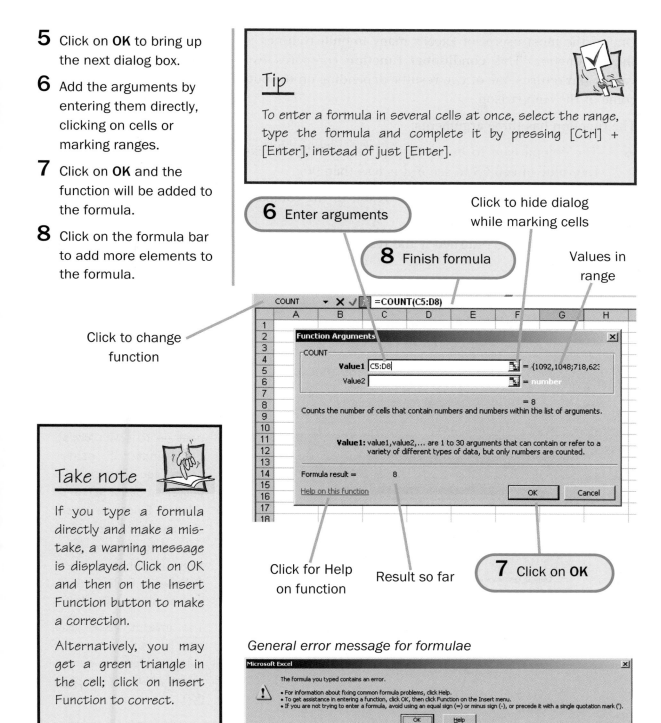

6 Enter arguments

Click to hide dialog while marking cells

8 Finish formula

Values in range

Click to change function

7 Click on **OK**

Click for Help on function

Result so far

Take note

If you type a formula directly and make a mistake, a warning message is displayed. Click on OK and then on the Insert Function button to make a correction.

Alternatively, you may get a green triangle in the cell; click on Insert Function to correct.

General error message for formulae

The IF function

One of the most useful of Excel's many in-built routines is the **IF** function. This **conditional function** compares two values and returns one of two results, depending on the outcome of the comparison.

The function has three arguments:

◆ The comparison to be performed (e.g. **C5<90** checks the value of cell C5 to see if it is less than 90);

◆ The value to be returned if the result of the comparison is true;

◆ The value to be returned if the result of the comparison is false.

The two return values may be constant values, text or further expressions.

Current values

COUNT	▼ X ✓ ƒ	=IF(B5>100,0.1,0.05)						
	A	B	C	D	E	F	G	H

Function Arguments ⊠

IF
Logical_test [B5>100] = TRUE
Value_if_true [0.1] = 0.1
Value_if_false [0.05] = 0.05

= 0.1

Checks whether a condition is met, and returns one value if TRUE, and another value if FALSE.

Logical_test is any value or expression that can be evaluated to TRUE or FALSE.

Formula result =   0.10

Help on this function   [OK]   [Cancel]

Current result

Operators

The following operators can be used in a comparison:

<	Less than
<=	Less than or equal
>	Greater than
>=	Greater than or equal
=	Equal
<>	Not equal

The **IF** function is included in the **Logical** category.

Tip

Although you can nest one IF statement inside another (in fact, you can nest up to seven levels), don't make IF statements too complex. It is better to use a series of related functions where the result in one cell is passed to the next function in another cell. Otherwise, finding errors becomes very difficult.

The intermediate cells can be put in rows or columns that are subsequently hidden (see page 52).

Logical functions

Comparison expressions can be combined with the following logical functions:

AND True if both expressions are true

OR True if either or both expressions are true

For example:

=IF(AND(A1 > 0 , B1 > 0), "Pos", "Neg")

The value 'Pos' is displayed only when both A1 and B1 are positive.

You can also use the **NOT** function, which reverses the result.

In the first illustration below, the Discount % column has a value of 0.10 if the Quantity is greater than 100, or 0.05 otherwise. The formula in E5 is:

=IF(B5>100, 0.1, 0.05)

This formula is copied over the range E6:E8. (See **page 42** for instructions on how to copy a formula.)

Complex decisions can be made by nesting **IF** functions. For instance, the discount calculation in the second illustration contains the formula in E8:

=IF(Discount_Rate=0,0,IF(Discount_Rate=1,0.1,0.05))

If the cell named Discount_Rate has a value of 0, the value returned is 0; otherwise, a further test is carried out, with a rate of 1 returning 0.1 and anything else giving 0.05.

You can also use the **IF** function to return warning messages if an input value is outside a permitted range.

The warning triangles tell you that the formulae are inconsistent with those near them – not a problem in this case

Formula in E5:

IF(B5>100, 0.1, 0.05)

	A	B	C	D	E	F	G	H
1								
2								
3		Quantity	Unit Price	Sub-total	Discount %	Discount	Total	
4								
5		120	2.32	278.40	0.10	27.84	250.56	
6		86	3.45	296.70	0.05	14.84	281.87	
7		100	1.28	128.00	0.05	6.40	121.60	
8		200	0.95	190.00	0.10	19.00	171.00	
9								
10								

Formula in E8:

IF(Discount_Rate=0, 0, IF(Discount_Rate=1, 0.1, 0.05))

	A	B	C	D	E	F	G
1							
2							
3			Discount Rate	1	(Enter 0, 1 or 2)		
4							
5							
6		Quantity	Unit Price	Sub-total	Discount %	Discount	Total
7							
8		120	2.32	278.40	0.10	27.84	250.56
9		86	3.45	296.70	0.10	29.67	267.03
10		100	1.28	128.00	0.10	12.80	115.20
11		200	0.95	190.00	0.10	19.00	171.00
12							
13							

Copying formulae

In most worksheets, you will need to repeat the same formula in a number of cells or fill a range with a similar formula. Excel makes it very easy for you to copy a formula to other cells.

In the example, the formula in C9 is =**SUM(C5:C8)**; this can be copied to D9. Excel does not make an exact duplicate of the formula; it assumes that the copied formula will refer to cells in the same **relative** position. That is, it sees the formula in C9 as an instruction to add together the contents of the four cells above. When the formula is copied, the effect is the same; the new formula adds together the cells above, becoming **SUM(D5:D8)**.

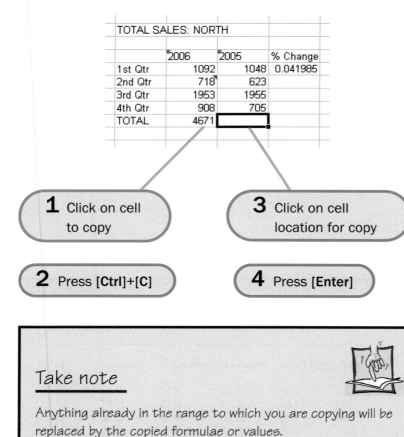

1 Click on cell to copy

2 Press [**Ctrl**]+[**C**]

3 Click on cell location for copy

4 Press [**Enter**]

Basic steps

- **To copy a single formula:**

1 Click on the cell to be copied, so that it is highlighted.

2 Press [**Ctrl**]+[**C**] to copy the formula to the Windows **Clipboard** (or select **Edit > Copy**).

3 Click on the cell where the copy is to appear, or drag the pointer to highlight a range of cells.

4 Press [**Enter**] (or select **Edit > Paste**). The formula will be repeated in each of the highlighted cells.

You can make several copies of the same cell if you use **Edit > Paste** instead of [**Enter**].

- **To copy a range of cells:**

1 Mark the range to be copied.

2 Press **[Ctrl]+[C]** to copy all the formulae to the **Clipboard**.

3 Click on the cell that will be in the top left-hand corner when the range is copied. (You can also mark a range that will take multiple copies of the original range, providing it is exactly the right size and shape.)

4 Press **[Enter]** to complete the copy.

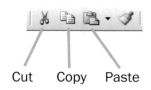

Cut   Copy   Paste

Edit options

(you may have to add these to the toolbar by clicking on the >> button)

Shortcuts

Cut   **[Ctrl] + [X]**

Copy   **[Ctrl] + [C]**

Paste   **[Ctrl] + [V]**

The % Change formula in E5 can be copied down the column by clicking on E5, pressing **[Ctrl]+[C]**, dragging over the range E6:E9 and pressing **[Enter]**.

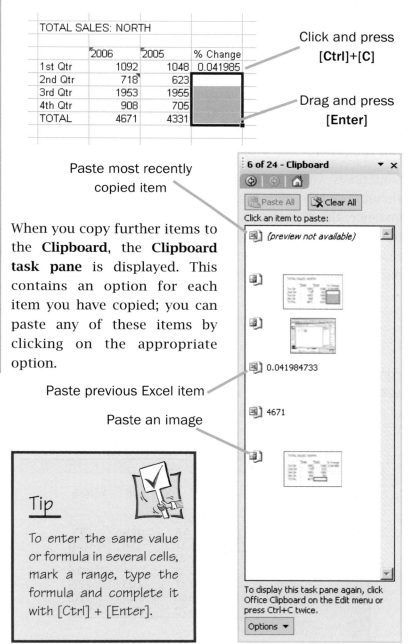

Click and press **[Ctrl]+[C]**

Drag and press **[Enter]**

Paste most recently copied item

When you copy further items to the **Clipboard**, the **Clipboard task pane** is displayed. This contains an option for each item you have copied; you can paste any of these items by clicking on the appropriate option.

Paste previous Excel item

Paste an image

Tip

To enter the same value or formula in several cells, mark a range, type the formula and complete it with [Ctrl] + [Enter].

Relative and absolute

When you copy a formula to another cell, any cell references are automatically updated so that they refer to the cell in the same relative position; these are called **relative cell references**.

Often, you want the formula to refer to the **same** cell, regardless of where the formula is copied. For instance, an invoice may take the discount rate from a single cell. To do this, each part of the cell reference is preceded by a $ sign; for example, a formula that refers to $C$24 will always use the value in C24, no matter where it is copied to. This is an **absolute cell reference**.

Sometimes you need to keep one part of the reference absolute while allowing the other part to change. For instance, the items in a table may be based on the values at the top of each column or on the left of each row. In these cases, the $ sign is placed in front of the part that is to remain unchanged. These are **mixed cell references**.

Options

Suppose that a formula in C54 referring to C24 is copied over the range C54:D56. There are four possible combinations for the reference in the new formulae:

- For a relative reference, both parts are changed when the formula is copied (e.g. C24 becomes C25, C26, D24, D25, D26).

- For an absolute reference, nothing changes (e.g. $C$24 stays as $C$24 no matter where it is copied).

- If the column is fixed, only the row number changes (e.g. $C24 becomes $C25, $C26, $C24, $C25, $C26).

- If the row is fixed, only the column letter changes (e.g. C$24 becomes C$24, C$24, D$24, D$24, D$24).

Formula in C6 uses three types of reference   Mixed ref: Column B fixed   Mixed ref: Row 5 fixed   Absolute reference

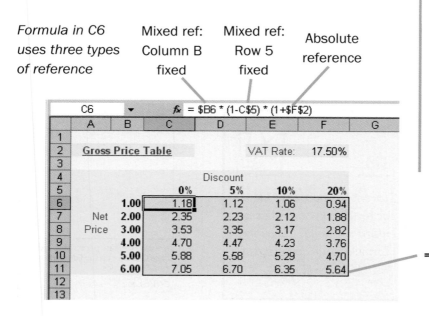

C6 f_x = $B6 * (1-C$5) * (1+$F$2)

	A	B	C	D	E	F	G
1							
2		Gross Price Table			VAT Rate:	17.50%	
3							
4					Discount		
5				0%	5%	10%	20%
6		1.00	1.18	1.12	1.06	0.94	
7	Net	2.00	2.35	2.23	2.12	1.88	
8	Price	3.00	3.53	3.35	3.17	2.82	
9		4.00	4.70	4.47	4.23	3.76	
10		5.00	5.88	5.58	5.29	4.70	
11		6.00	7.05	6.70	6.35	5.64	
12							
13							

Formula in F11:
= **$B11 * (1-F$5) * (1+$F$2)**

Moving cells and ranges

1 Click on the cell
or drag over the range.

2 Press [Ctrl]+[X] to cut the
highlighted area to the
Clipboard (the cells are
cleared).

3 Click on the cell that is to
be the top left-hand
corner of the range.

4 Press [Enter]. The
contents of the cell or
range appear in their new
position.

As an alternative to copying the contents of cells (so that you have multiple copies), you can move the contents to a new location (clearing out the originals).

The principles are similar to those for copying but you will end up with a single copy of the original range in a new position.

Tip

When a formula is moved, the cell references are not updated (unlike the effect when a formula is copied). If you want the references changed, you should copy the formula and then delete the original.

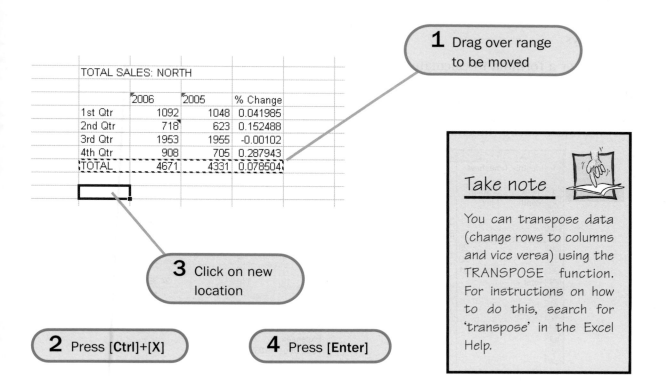

1 Drag over range to be moved

TOTAL SALES: NORTH

	2006	2005	% Change
1st Qtr	1092	1048	0.041985
2nd Qtr	718	623	0.152488
3rd Qtr	1953	1955	-0.00102
4th Qtr	908	705	0.287943
TOTAL	4671	4331	0.078504

3 Click on new location

2 Press [Ctrl]+[X]

4 Press [Enter]

Take note

You can transpose data (change rows to columns and vice versa) using the TRANSPOSE function. For instructions on how to do this, search for 'transpose' in the Excel Help.

Exercises

1 Create a worksheet for calculating VAT. Save the file as VATCalculator.xls.

	A	B	C	D	E
1					
2					
3		Amount	12.48		
4					
5		VAT Rate	0.175		
6		VAT	2.184		
7					
8		Total	14.664		
9					
10					

2 Enter formula to calculate the VAT and Total. Test the worksheet.

3 Add names to each value in column C and rewrite the formulae to include the names. Close the worksheet.

4 Open the Timesheet.xls worksheet from Chapter 2. Enter a formula in G8 (using the **SUM** function) to calculate the total hours for the first day.

5 Copy the formula down the column for the other 30 days.

6 Enter a formula to calculate the total in C39 and copy it to D39:G39 and I39.

7 Enter formulae to calculate the values in G41 and G43:G45. Save the changes.

	A	B	C	D	E	F	G	H	I
1	Monthly Timesheet								2006
2									
3	Name:	J Smith							
4	Month:	May							
5									
6			Hours					Expenses	
7	Date		Project 1	Project 2	Project 3	Project 4	TOTAL	Details	Amount
36		29					0		
37		30	3	4		1	8		
38		31					0		
39	Total		66	39	24	19	148		24.35
40									
41				SUMMARY		Hours	148		
42						x Rate	7		
43						Pay	1036		
44						Expenses	24.35		
45						Total Due	1060.35		
46									

4 Sheet formatting

Columns and rows

Entering values and formulae is only the start of using a worksheet. Usually, you will be aiming to produce some type of report from it or, at the very least, will want to improve the layout of the sheet for your own benefit.

The first stage is to change the widths of the columns to make them more suitable for the data they contain. By default, each column starts with a column width of about nine numeric characters. You can change this default – so that all columns take this new width – or you can adjust individual columns.

You can adjust either a single column or a marked range of columns. The change can be made either by selecting the appropriate menu option or by dragging the dividers between columns or rows.

Width options

- Select **Format > Column > Standard Width** to set a new default width.

- Click on a cell or mark a range and then select **Format > Column > Width** to change the width of one or more columns.

- Select **Format > Column > AutoFit Selection** to make the width of one or more columns automatically adjust to fit the longest item of data in each case.

- Use the **Format Painter** to copy the width of one column to another (see **page 72**).

- Alternatively, you can change the column width using a shortcut (see opposite).

Take note

If you enter a date in a column that has the default width, the width is increased to accommodate the date.

Column width is given in terms of the average number of characters in the standard font

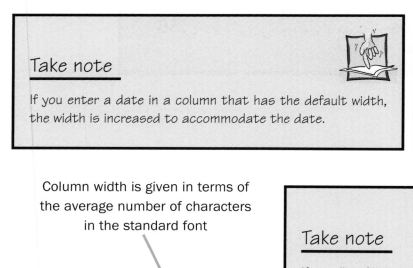

Take note

If a cell is filled with # characters, the column is not wide enough to display the numeric value held in the cell. Increasing the width will allow the number to be shown again.

Height options

- Select **Format > Row > Height** to change the height of a single row or a highlighted series of rows.

- Select **Format > Row > AutoFit** to make the height of the rows adjust to fit their contents.

- Alternatively, you can change the row height using a shortcut (see below).

In a similar way to the width, you can adjust the height of each row. This will be necessary if you change the fonts, use multi-line text, or simply want to put a bigger gap between sections of the worksheet.

Row height is given in points; there are 72 points per inch. The standard font uses 10-point text.

(The other 2.75 points provide a gap between lines of text.)

Shortcuts

- The quickest way to change the width of a single column is to drag the right-hand edge of the column border (next to the column letter). To make a column fit the widest item of data in that column, double-click on the column border.

- The easiest way to change the height of a row is to drag the bottom edge of the row border (immediately below the row number).

Double-click on border to make column fit widest item in column B

Drag here to change width of column A

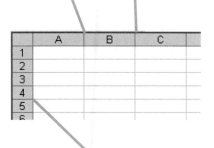

Drag here to change height of row 4

Take note

If you change the font used for a cell (see page 68), the row height is adjusted to suit the new font. Similarly, if text is formatted to be multi-line, any row that contains a cell where the text has been split over more than one line will expand to fit.

49

Creating gaps

You should always design the layout of the worksheet before you start to put anything on the computer but, inevitably, there will be times when you don't get it right first time. You can delete or move the contents of cells without any difficulty and you can insert or delete rows or columns.

New rows are inserted above the current row, new columns to the left of the current column, using the **Insert** menu.

1 Click on a cell.

2 Select **Rows** or **Columns** from the **Insert** menu.

For **Rows**, the new row is inserted above the current row; for **Columns**, the new column is inserted to the left of the current column.

To insert more than one row or column, highlight the required number of cells. For instance, to insert three blank rows, start by marking a range that covers three existing rows.

Insert rows

Insert columns

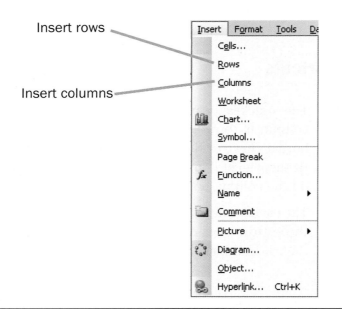

Insert	Format	Tools	Da
Cells...			
Rows			
Columns			
Worksheet			
Chart...			
Symbol...			
Page Break			
Function...			
Name		▶	
Comment			
Picture		▶	
Diagram...			
Object...			
Hyperlink...	Ctrl+K		

Tip

To insert a row or column quickly, right-click on the row number or column letter and select Insert from the pop-up menu.

To insert several rows or columns, highlight the required number of rows or columns before right-clicking.

Take note

All new columns have the same width and format as the column to the left, not the current column.

All formulae are updated so that they still relate to the same cells as before (regardless of whether the references were relative or absolute).

Deleting rows/columns

Rows and columns are erased from the worksheet with frightening simplicity. The **Edit > Delete** option lets you cut out any section of the sheet.

To delete the contents of a range without moving the cells to the right or below, mark the cells and press **[Delete]**.

1 Mark a range that covers all the rows or columns to be deleted.

2 Select **Delete** from the **Edit** menu; the **Delete** dialog box appears.

3 Click on **Entire row** to delete one or more rows, **Entire column** for the columns. (Alternatively, use **Shift cells left** or **Shift cells up** if you want to remove a block of cells.)

Delete a range and move adjacent cells to fill the gap

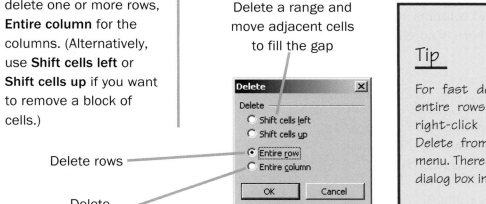

Delete rows

Delete columns

Tip

For fast deletion, mark entire rows or columns, right-click and select Delete from the pop-up menu. There is no warning dialog box in this case.

Tip

Always save the worksheet with [Ctrl]+[S] before deleting anything; it is very easy to make mistakes and deletions cannot always be undone.

Take note

After a deletion, all rows and columns are renumbered and all formulae are revised so that they still refer to the original cells.

If you delete a row or column that is part of a range reference, the formula will adjust; however, if you delete the whole of a range from a reference or an individual cell that is referenced, the result of the formula will be #REF! and the formula will have to be amended. A green triangle is added to the cell.

Hiding rows/columns

The results produced on worksheets often require a series of steps, with one or more intermediate values. These extra cells may clutter the display and be of no interest in themselves, once the sheet is working satisfactorily. Therefore the unwanted values can be placed in separate rows and columns, which can then be **hidden**.

The effect of hiding a row or column is simply that it does not appear on the display or in printouts; the formulae in hidden rows and columns still work in exactly the same way as before and there is no effect on the results.

- **To hide rows or columns:**

1 Mark a range that covers at least one cell in each of the rows or columns to be hidden.

2 Select **Format > Row > Hide** or **Format > Column > Hide**.

Alternatively, mark the complete columns, right-click and select **Hide**.

- **To redisplay rows/columns:**

1 Mark a range that includes cells either side of the hidden rows and columns.

2 Select **Format > Row > Unhide** or **Format > Column > Unhide**.

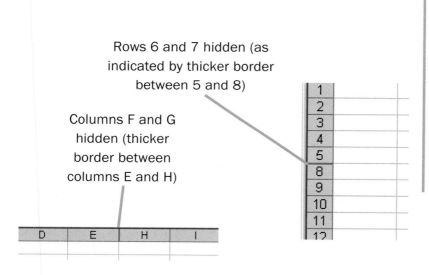

Rows 6 and 7 hidden (as indicated by thicker border between 5 and 8)

Columns F and G hidden (thicker border between columns E and H)

Tip

You can tell when there are hidden rows or columns on a worksheet because there will be a jump in the row numbers or column letters and there is a thicker border line between them.

Take note

The title bar, toolbars and status bar can be hidden (or redisplayed) using View > Full Screen. The Row & Column Headers option in the View tab of the Tools > Options command hides the row letters and column numbers.

Wildcards

Checking text

Two wildcards can be used with the **Find** option:

- ■ **?** represents any single character.

- ■ ***** represents any group of characters (or no characters).

For example, **jan*sales** will find 'Jan 2002 Sales', 'January Sales' and 'JanSales'.

The **Find** option in the **Edit** menu searches the worksheet for a specified piece of text. This may be a word, a phrase or just a few characters from a word. The search will be in both formulae and values, unless you specify **Values** (in which case formulae are ignored). The search is in the whole worksheet, unless you have marked a range.

The **Replace** option (which uses the **Replace** tab on the same dialog box) searches for one piece of text and then replaces it with another one.

Text to find

Search in formulae and values

Search for text with matching format

Hide/show options

Word not recognised

Suggested replacement

The **Spelling** option from the **Tools** menu checks all text in the worksheet against a built-in dictionary and displays any words it does not recognise, with suggested replacements.

Spelling checker

Options for ignoring or changing the unrecognised word

Language used for spell check

Sorting data

Sorting data is one of the easiest tasks you can perform in Excel, yet is powerful and has many uses.

Simple sorting involves marking a range and then clicking on one of the sort buttons, to sort the contents of the cells in either **ascending** (A to Z) or **descending** (Z to A) order. The contents of the cells are reorganised by the sort and any formulae that rely on these cells are updated accordingly. Any cells outside the marked range are unaffected by the sort.

If you mark more than one column, the cells in the first column are sorted and the cells in the other marked columns are moved as well, so that the data in each marked row stays the same.

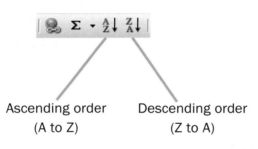

Ascending order
(A to Z)

Descending order
(Z to A)

Rules

- All numeric values come before text values and are sorted in order of magnitude.

- Numbers entered as text are sorted character by character (so '12' is before '3', because the character '1' comes before '3').

- Characters other than numbers and letters are first in the sort order, followed by numeric characters and then alphabetic letters.

- Upper and lower case letters are treated the same, unless you specify otherwise.

Tip

If you need to keep a note of the original order of the cells, number the cells to the right and then mark both columns before sorting. During the sort the cells are reorganised in pairs, so each number stays with the corresponding value.

Unsorted			Sorted	
Albert		-623	
(also)		0.999	
--- ends ---		3.14159	
aardvark		78	
125 train		128	
{yes}		--- ends ---	
A		(also)	
Beethoven	→	{yes}	
33 rpm		125 train	
beetroot		33 rpm	
128		A	
78		aardvark	
3.14159		Albert	
-623		Beethoven	
0.999		beetroot	

Basic steps

1 Mark the range to be sorted and select **Sort** from the **Data** menu.

2 Choose the columns on which the sort is to be based (selecting from the list of currently highlighted columns).

3 For each sort column, choose **Ascending** or **Descending** order.

4 Specify whether or not there is a **header row**. (The header row is not included in the sort.)

5 Click on the **Options** button to further refine the sort. Click on **OK** to close the **Sort Options** dialog box.

6 Click on **OK** to perform the sort.

For a more sophisticated sort, select **Sort** from the **Data** menu. This allows you to choose up to three columns for sorting. If the entries in the first sort column are the same, the sort is based on the second column; if these are also identical, the order is determined by the third column.

You can choose ascending or descending order for each column independently, and also make the sort case-sensitive (with capitals before lower-case letters).

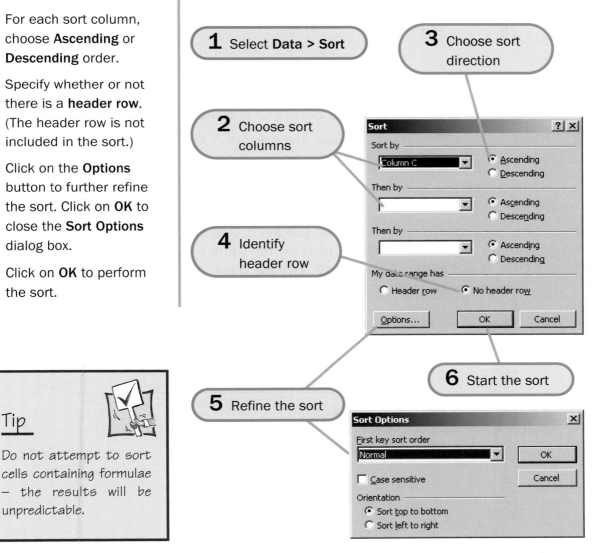

1 Select **Data > Sort**

2 Choose sort columns

3 Choose sort direction

4 Identify header row

5 Refine the sort

6 Start the sort

Tip

Do not attempt to sort cells containing formulae – the results will be unpredictable.

55

Exercises

1   Open the VATCalculator.xls sheet from Chapter 3. Insert a column after column B.

2   Enter the values shown below in F3:H4.

	A	B	C	D	E	F	G	H	I
1									
2									
3		Amount		12.48		0	1	2	
4						0	0.05	0.175	
5		VAT Rate	2	0.175		0	0	0.175	
6		VAT		2.184					
7									
8		Total		14.664					
9									

3   Enter a formula in F5 that returns the value in F4 if C5 is the same as F3, otherwise 0. (Use the **IF** function and a relative reference.) Copy the formula to G5 and G6.

4   Enter a formula in D5 that shows the selected VAT rate.

5   Hide columns F, G and H. Save and close the worksheet.

6   Open the Timesheet.xls sheet from Chapter 3. Reduce the width of columns A and B. Increase the width of column H and the height of row 39. Save the sheet.

	A	B	C	D	E	F	G	H	I	J
1	Monthly Timesheet								2006	
2										
3	Name:	J Smith								
4	Month:	May								
5										
6			Hours					Expenses		
7	Date		Project 1	Project 2	Project 3	Project 4	TOTAL	Details	Amount	
36		29					0			
37		30	3	4		1	8			
38		31					0			
39	Total		66	39	24	19	148		24.35	
40										
41				SUMMARY		Hours	148			
42						x Rate	7			
43						Pay	1036			
44						Expenses	24.35			
45						Total Due	1060.35			

5 Formatting cells

Number formats

Up until this point, numeric values have been displayed with the format that best suits them in each individual case: as whole numbers; with a limited number of decimal places; or using scientific format. This is the **General** format and you will usually want to change it in different parts of the worksheet. For example, monetary values will usually be displayed with exactly two decimal places; alternatively, you may want to round the results of calculations to the nearest whole number or a specific number of places after the decimal point.

The format for a cell or range is altered using the **Format > Cells** option.

Basic steps

1 Click on the cell to be formatted or mark a range of cells.

2 Select **Cells** from the **Format** menu (or right-click and select **Format Cells**), then click on the **Number** tab.

3 Choose the category that applies to the type of data being formatted.

4 Select the precise format, depending on category (e.g. for the **Number** category, select the number of decimal places, whether or not to use a thousands separator, and how to handle negative numbers).

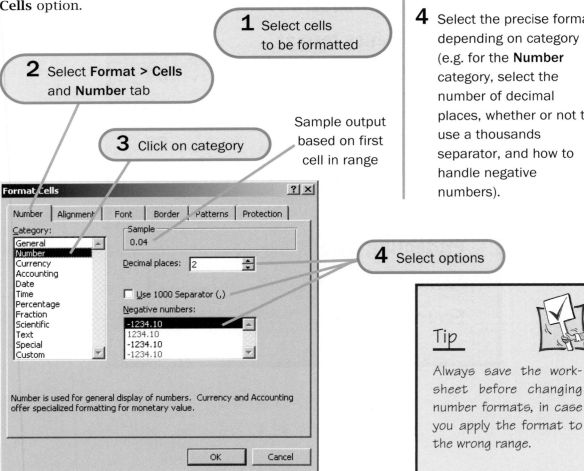

1 Select cells to be formatted

2 Select **Format > Cells** and **Number** tab

3 Click on category

Sample output based on first cell in range

Format Cells [?][x]

| Number | Alignment | Font | Border | Patterns | Protection |

Category:
- General
- **Number**
- Currency
- Accounting
- Date
- Time
- Percentage
- Fraction
- Scientific
- Text
- Special
- Custom

Sample
0.04

Decimal places: 2

☐ Use 1000 Separator (,)

Negative numbers:
- -1234.10
- 1234.10
- -1234.10
- -1234.10

4 Select options

Number is used for general display of numbers. Currency and Accounting offer specialized formatting for monetary value.

OK   Cancel

Tip

Always save the worksheet before changing number formats, in case you apply the format to the wrong range.

58

Format options

- **Number** formats include integers (whole numbers) and various levels of decimal places.

- **Currency** formats are similar to **Number** formats but insert a symbol at the front of the displayed number.

- **Date** and **Time** formats provide several alternatives for the display of date and time values (see **page 64**).

- **Percentage** formats convert all values to percentages.

- **Fraction** formats allow you to display fractions rather than decimals (e.g. 40/47 instead of 0.851).

- **Scientific** formats use the exponential style (see the Excel Help for details).

- **Accounting** formats are similar to **Number** formats but use a dash to represent zero values.

- **Custom** formats display data according to rules you specify (see the Excel Help for details).

When you choose a number format, the Sample line in the dialog box shows you what the first highlighted cell will look like when it is displayed.

A wide range of possible formats is built into the system.

TOTAL SALES: NORTH			
	2006	2005	% Change
1st Qtr	1092	1048	4.20%
2nd Qtr	718	623	15.25%
3rd Qtr	1953	1955	-0.10%
4th Qtr	908	705	28.79%
TOTAL	4671	4331	7.85%

Percentage format with 2 decimal places

You can also devise your own format. For example, you might want to display all negative values in red. This is done by creating a **Custom** format, for which you specify the display style for positive numbers, negative numbers, zero values and text. For information on how to create a **Custom** format, search for 'custom format' in the Excel Help.

Tip

Depending on the format you choose, Excel will add to the display value a monetary symbol (e.g. £), commas to separate thousands, % signs, and a minus sign or brackets for negative numbers. Although you can use these symbols when entering data, you cannot do so when entering formulae. Therefore, it is best not to enter the characters £ , % () yourself but let Excel apply them as appropriate. (Always indicate negative values with a − sign.)

Decimal places

In most cases you will want to restrict the number of decimal places used in displayed values. The various formats on offer limit the number of figures after the decimal point.

◆ The **integer** format displays values as whole numbers (select the **Number** category with **0** decimal places).

◆ The various **floating point** formats (also in the **Number** category) give an exact number of decimal places; if necessary, extra 0s are added at the end to pad out the number.

◆ The **Percentage** format can be a bit confusing; formatting 0.175 as a percentage results in a display of '17.5%'.

◆ The **Currency** format works like a floating point value but inserts a currency symbol (e.g. £).

◆ The **Custom** format gives you complete control over the display style (see the Excel Help for details).

(Note that values are stored with 15 significant figures, which includes all figures before and after the decimal point.)

Tip

Do not use more decimal places than are reasonable or necessary. For instance, with monetary values there is rarely a need for more than two decimal places.

Take note

The General format displays up to nine decimal places.

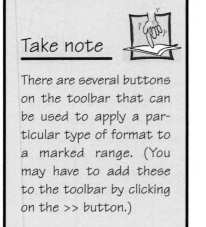

Take note

There are several buttons on the toolbar that can be used to apply a particular type of format to a marked range. (You may have to add these to the toolbar by clicking on the >> button.)

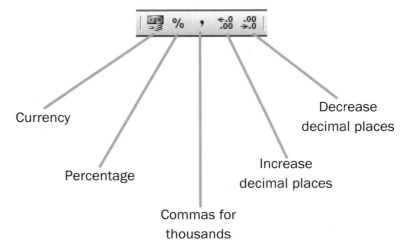

Currency

Percentage

Commas for thousands

Increase decimal places

Decrease decimal places

Displayed values

Precision as displayed

Sometimes you want the stored value to match the displayed value: for example, most calculations involving money will need the result stored to the nearest penny and not with a dozen decimal places!

The **Tools > Options > Calculation > Precision As Displayed** option permanently changes stored values so that they match the displayed amounts.

When the **General** format is applied, the displayed value will have as many decimal places as are necessary for the value on screen to match that stored in memory (providing the column is wide enough). The value in any cell, whether entered directly or calculated from a formula, is stored in memory with 15 significant figures.

However, as soon as a different format is applied, with the number of decimal places limited, the value will be rounded for the display. For example, with an integer display format, any value ending in 0.5 or more will be rounded **up** to the next whole number while those less than 0.5 are rounded **down**. Thus 3.5, 3.501 and 3.95 are all rounded up to 4 but 3.01, 3.45 and 3.49995 are all rounded down to 3.

The most important point is that all calculations use the **stored** value, rather than the **displayed** value. This can lead to some surprising results in the display, particularly when the results of formulae are added or subtracted.

> ## Take note
>
> Precision As Displayed applies to all cells in the current file, so should be used with care. In complex calculations, rounding errors can accumulate rapidly.

Formula	Actual value	Integer display	Comments
A	2.45	2	
B	2.35	2	
C = A + B	4.8	5	2 + 2 = 5 !
D = C * 3	14.4	14	5 * 3 = 14 !

Rounding may produce unexpected results (particular if the intermediate values are hidden)

> ## Tip
>
> Use the INT function to round a value to a particular number of decimal places. For example, =(INT(A1 * 100 + 0.5)) / 100 stores the number in A1 to two decimal places.

The Currency format

The **Currency** format inserts a currency symbol in front of each value. You can choose either the default symbol (which will depend on the regional settings applied to Windows on your computer) or some other symbol from the drop-down list.

Sample shows how current cell will appear

Format Cells   ? X

| Number | Alignment | Font | Border | Patterns | Protection |

Category:

General
Number
Currency
Accounting
Date
Time
Percentage
Fraction
Scientific
Text
Special
Custom

Sample
£4.14

Decimal places: 2

Symbol:
£

None
£
₮ Mongolian (Cyrillic)
$ English (Australia)
$ English (Canada)
$ English (Caribbean)
$ English (New Zealand)
$ English (United States)
$ French (Canada)

Currency formats are used for general monetary values. Use Accounting formats to align decimal points in a column.

OK   Cancel

Click to choose currency symbol from drop-down list

Default currency symbol shown at top of list

Symbol:
☐ Euro (☐ 123)

$ English (Caribbean)
$ English (New Zealand)
$ English (United States)
$ French (Canadian)
$ Spanish (Argentina)
£ English (British)
☐ Euro (☐ 123)
☐ Euro (123 ☐)
B Spanish (Panama)

Empty square box indicates euro symbol not supported

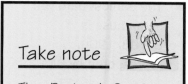

When you mark a part of the worksheet with the default **Currency** format you may find that the values are displayed with $ at the front rather than £ (or other local currency). In this case, Windows is not set up for UK (or other national) use; the currency symbol is a function of Windows, rather than Excel.

To change the symbol, double-click on the **Regional and Language Options** icon in the Windows **Control Panel** (selected from the Windows **Start** menu). Then click on the **Regional Options** tab, choose a region and click on **OK**. (Although the defaults offered by Windows should be satisfactory, you can click on the **Customize** button to change features such as the currency symbol.) As soon as you get back to Excel, the display will be updated.

Click to change any format

Regional and Language Options   ? X

Regional Options | Languages | Advanced

Standards and formats

This option affects how some programs format numbers, currencies, dates, and time.

Select an item to match its preferences, or click Customize to choose your own formats:

English (United Kingdom) ▼   Customize...

Samples

Number: 123,456,789.00

Currency: £123,456,789.00

Time: 14:07:11

Short date: 09/05/2006

Long date: 09 May 2006

Location

To help services provide you with local information, such as news and weather, select your present location:

United Kingdom ▼

OK   Cancel   Apply

Select the region to be used in all programs

Samples show how numbers, times and dates will be displayed – click on **Customize** to change these formats

Dates and times

Excel can handle dates and times in calculations. It does this by storing any date or time as a numeric value, rather than as text.

Dates are stored as integers, representing the number of days since 30th December 1899. For example, 36526 represents 1st January 2000.

If you enter a date in the **General** format, Excel displays it in the form dd/mm/yyyy. If this is then copied to another cell and formatted as an integer, the number that represents that date will be shown. Similarly, an integer formatted as a date will show in date format provided it is within the permissible range.

	A	B	C	D	E
1					
2		Date	26/08/2006		
3		Date value	38955		=C2, formatted as a number
4					
5		Time	4:00 AM		
6		Time value	0.17		=C5, formatted as a number (2 dp)
7					
8		Value	38929.17		
9		Date & Time	31/07/2006 04:04		=C8, formatted as dd/mm/yyyy hh:mm
10					
11					

Select from **Custom** category
in **Format Cells** dialog

Limits

- The earliest date you should use is 01/03/1900, represented by 61.

- The latest recognised date is 31/12/9999, represented by 2,958,465.

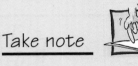

Take note

The values for dates before March 1900 are wrong, as Excel incorrectly treats 1900 as a leap year.

If you need to use dates earlier than this you will have to adjust any formulae accordingly. To get the correct value, add 1.

Tip

A date that has been entered as text can be converted to its numeric value with the DATEVALUE function. The DAY, MONTH and YEAR functions extract the relevant portions of a date (which may be held either in date format or as a number). WEEKDAY returns the day of the week as a number: 1 is Sunday, 7 is Saturday.

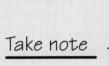

Take note

Earlier versions of Excel had a limit for dates of 31/12/2078.

Excel does not allow you to use negative numbers for dates before 1900.

The following functions can be used to derive values from the system clock:

- **TODAY** returns the current date.

- **NOW** returns the current date and time.

In a similar way, time of day is stored as a number in the range 0 to 1, with the value representing the portion of the day that has elapsed. So 6 a.m. is represented by 0.25, mid-day is 0.5 and midnight is 0.

Numbers and times (including AM and PM if required) can be interchanged by applying numeric or time formats.

You can also combine a date and time; the part to the left of the decimal place represents the date, that to the right represents the time. For instance, the value 36526.25 represents 1-Jan-2000 6:00 AM.

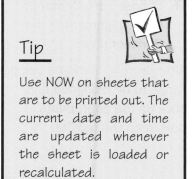
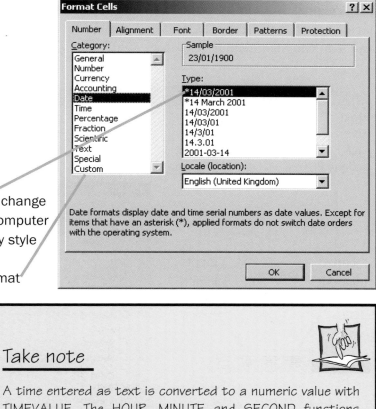

Asterisk indicates date format may change if spreadsheet loaded on another computer – use **Custom** format to fix display style

Custom format

Printed on:
09/05/2006 14:27

=**NOW**()

Alignment

When data is first entered, text is placed on the left of the cell and numbers line up on the right. Numbers can be tidied up by applying a suitable format: for example, a fixed number of decimal places. For most purposes this is satisfactory but there are times when you need the text to be aligned to the right of the cell or the numbers on the left.

The **Format > Cells** command has an **Alignment** tab that allows you to change the position of data in any cell. As a shortcut, four of the buttons on the toolbar can be used to apply a new alignment to the range that is currently highlighted.

The **Vertical** options on the **Alignment** tab allow you to decide whether the text is at the top, bottom or middle of the row. You can also display text at an angle.

Basic steps

1 Mark the cell, range, row or column to be realigned.

2 Select **Cells** from the **Format** menu (or right-click and select **Format Cells**).

3 Click on the **Alignment** tab.

4 Choose **Left**, **Center** or **Right** alignment in the **Horizontal** box.

Alternatively, mark the cell or range to be realigned and click on the appropriate button on the toolbar.

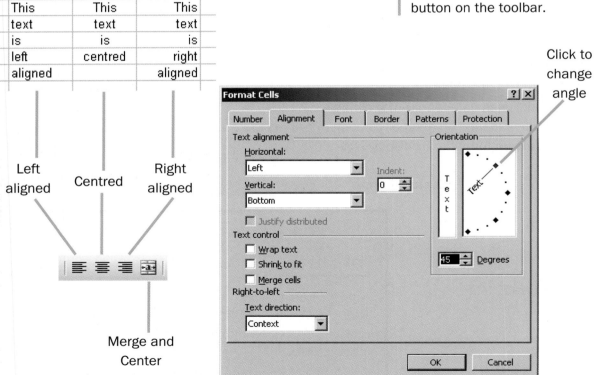

This	This	This
text	text	text
is	is	is
left	centred	right
aligned		aligned

Left aligned   Centred   Right aligned

Merge and Center

Click to change angle

Basic steps

- **To centre an item of text over several columns:**

1 Type the text into the left-hand column.

2 Mark a range, starting with the text cell and extending over the cells in which the text is to be centred. (All cells apart from the first must be empty.)

3 Select **Format > Cells** and choose **Center Across Selection** from the **Horizontal** list on the **Alignment** tab.

You can also use the **Merge and Center** button on the toolbar but this has a more permanent effect, merging the selected cells into a single cell.

Text can spread over more than one column or row.

◆ If you type text into a cell that is too narrow, and the cell to the right is empty, the text will spread over both columns on the display.

◆ Text can be **centred** over a group of cells, providing these are all blank, by setting the **Horizontal** alignment to **Center Across Selection**.

◆ Text can be made to **wrap** over multiple lines within a cell, using the **Wrap Text** option from the **Alignment** tab. Any words that will not fit on one line are carried over to the next line and the height of the row adjusts to take all the text.

◆ Text that has been wrapped in a cell can be **justified**, so that there is a straight right-hand margin; use the **Justify** option from the **Horizontal** drop-down list.

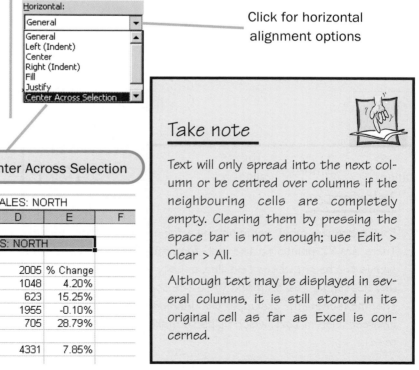

Click for horizontal alignment options

2 Mark range

3 Center Across Selection

Take note

Text will only spread into the next column or be centred over columns if the neighbouring cells are completely empty. Clearing them by pressing the space bar is not enough; use Edit > Clear > All.

Although text may be displayed in several columns, it is still stored in its original cell as far as Excel is concerned.

Changing fonts

The **font** is the style of text used to display the contents of cells (both text and numeric values). A font is defined by the following characteristics:

◆ The **typeface** (e.g. Arial, Times and Courier)

◆ The **point size** (e.g. 8-point, 10-point and 12-point)

◆ The **attributes** (e.g. **bold**, *italic* and underline)

Fonts are applied to cells and ranges in a similar way to other characteristics, such as alignment. Although you can use the **Font** tab from the **Format > Cells** command, the easiest way is to use the buttons on the toolbar.

The default font is 10-point Arial, with no attributes set.

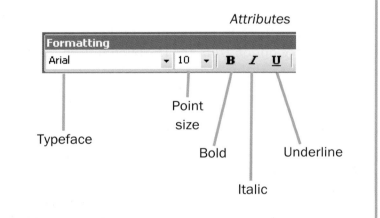

Attributes

Typeface

Point size

Bold

Italic

Underline

Basic steps

■ **To change the font for cells:**

1 Select the cell or range to which the new font is to be applied.

2 Click on the arrow to the right of the typeface box on the toolbar and click on the required typeface from the drop-down list.

3 In a similar way, select the point size (or simply type the size directly into the **Point Size** box).

4 Click on the bold, italic or underline buttons to change the attributes. Each time you click a button, the attribute is turned on or off. Any combination of attributes is allowed. When an attribute is on, the corresponding button is shown in paler grey.

Tip

The Normal font box on the Format Cells dialog box returns the font, point size and attributes to the defaults.

Basic steps

- **To change the font for a group of characters:**

1 Double-click on the cell containing the text (for text centred across columns, the left-hand cell of the range).

2 Drag the pointer over the characters to be changed, highlighting them.

3 Select the typeface, size and attributes, as before.

The following keys are shortcuts for the attributes:

[Ctrl]+[B]   Bold

[Ctrl]+[I]   Italic

[Ctrl]+[U]   Underline

You can use these shortcuts either when changing the font inside a cell or when setting the font for a whole cell.

For cells formatted as numbers or dates, the font applies to all the characters in the cell. For text cells, however, you can format individual characters and groups of characters. This allows you to produce a mixture of fonts within a cell and is particularly useful for headings.

In the example below, the first character of each word in the main title has been formatted with a larger point size.

22-point bold

14-point bold

10-point bold right-aligned

	A	B	C	D	E	F
1						
2		**TOTAL SALES: NORTH**				
3						
4			2006	2005	% Change	
5		1st Qtr	1092	1048	4.20%	
6		2nd Qtr	718	623	15.25%	
7		3rd Qtr	1953	1955	-0.10%	
8		4th Qtr	908	705	28.79%	
9						
10		TOTAL	4671	4331	7.85%	
11						

Increased column width

Take note

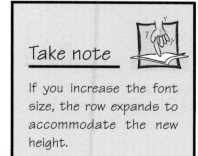

If you increase the font size, the row expands to accommodate the new height.

Tip

Use fonts sparingly; too many fonts on a worksheet or printed report look untidy and detract from the information you are trying to present. Apply different fonts to emphasise and enhance titles and results but keep the number of variations to a minimum.

Borders and patterns

For further enhancement of your work, and to highlight particular blocks of data or subdivide complicated tables, Excel provides a range of features for drawing boxes, shading cells and changing the colours.

Options

There are two ways of changing these features for the current cell or a highlighted range:

- Select the **Format > Cells** option, then click on the **Border**, **Patterns** or **Font** tab.

- Click on the arrows to the right of the borders, fill colour and font colour buttons on the toolbar, then select from the drop-down lists.

When a border, colour or pattern has been chosen, it can be applied to further cells or ranges by selecting the area to be changed and clicking on the appropriate button again.

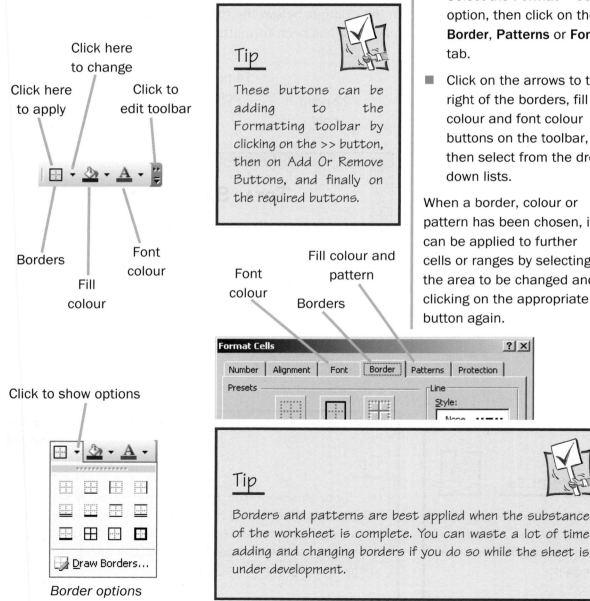

Click here to change

Click here to apply

Click to edit toolbar

Borders

Fill colour

Font colour

Tip

These buttons can be adding to the Formatting toolbar by clicking on the >> button, then on Add Or Remove Buttons, and finally on the required buttons.

Font colour

Fill colour and pattern

Borders

Click to show options

Border options

Tip

Borders and patterns are best applied when the substance of the worksheet is complete. You can waste a lot of time adding and changing borders if you do so while the sheet is under development.

Borders, patterns and colours can be applied to individual cells or ranges.

◆ To draw a border around a block of cells, highlight the entire block, then choose the border.

◆ To divide columns with vertical lines, mark each column separately and apply a border on the right (or left).

◆ To box individual cells, each cell must be given its own border. The border can also be applied to individual edges of each cell.

The background colour is applied to whole cells. In the same way as for fonts, the text colour can be changed for individual characters in a text cell but must be applied to the entire cell for numbers and dates.

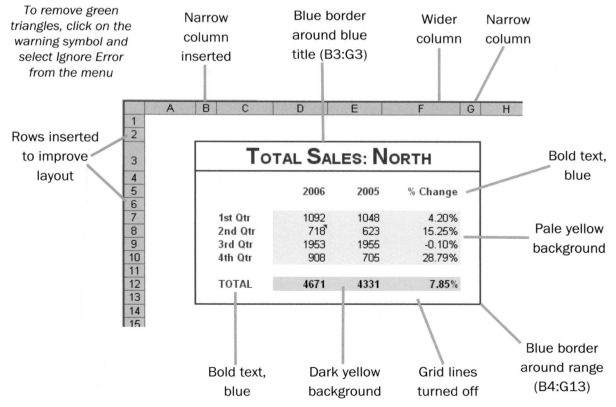

To remove green triangles, click on the warning symbol and select Ignore Error from the menu

Narrow column inserted

Blue border around blue title (B3:G3)

Wider column

Narrow column

Rows inserted to improve layout

Bold text, blue

Pale yellow background

	2006	2005	% Change
1st Qtr	1092	1048	4.20%
2nd Qtr	718	623	15.25%
3rd Qtr	1953	1955	-0.10%
4th Qtr	908	705	28.79%
TOTAL	4671	4331	7.85%

TOTAL SALES: NORTH

Bold text, blue

Dark yellow background

Grid lines turned off

Blue border around range (B4:G13)

Copying formats

When you have created a display format for one cell, you can easily copy this to any other range on the worksheet using the **Format Painter**. This will apply the same number/text format, alignment, font, border, pattern and colour to all selected cells.

You can also copy the format of an entire row or column. If you mark a row by clicking on the row number, click on the **Format Painter** button and then click on another row number (or drag over several rows), the format will be copied, including the row height. Similarly, you can use the **Format Painter** to copy the format for a column, including column width.

If you are going to use the same formats regularly, then it is worth setting up some **format styles** – see **page 74**.

1 Click on the cell whose format is to be copied.

2 Click on the **Format Painter** button.

3 Mark the range that is to receive the new format.

When the mouse button is released, the new format is applied to all the highlighted cells, replacing whatever was there before.

You can undo most mistakes in formatting with **[Ctrl]+[Z]** but you should always save a copy of the worksheet before you start, as you may not always be able to get the sheet back to its original format.

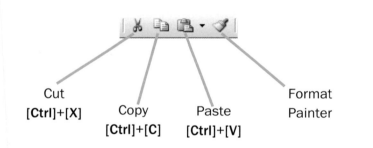

Cut
[Ctrl]+[X]

Copy
[Ctrl]+[C]

Paste
[Ctrl]+[V]

Format
Painter

Take note

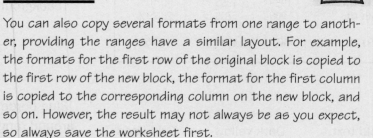

You can also copy several formats from one range to another, providing the ranges have a similar layout. For example, the formats for the first row of the original block is copied to the first row of the new block, the format for the first column is copied to the corresponding column on the new block, and so on. However, the result may not always be as you expect, so always save the worksheet first.

Tip

To copy the format to several ranges, mark the original range and double-click on the Format Painter button. Mark each of the required ranges, then click the button again to turn the Format Painter off.

Protecting data

Basic steps

1 Mark a range of cells in which data entry is to be allowed. (Click on a column letter or row number to mark a whole column or row.)

2 Select **Format > Cells**, click on the **Protection Tab** and clear the **Locked** box.

3 Repeat for other ranges not to be protected.

4 Select **Tools > Protection > Protect Sheet**. Enter a password if required (make sure [**Caps Lock**] is off so that the password is not inadvertently in capitals). Click on **OK**.

Clear the protection with **Tools > Protection > Unprotect Sheet**.

Much of the sheet will contain data that is to be derived from formulae and therefore must not be changed directly. You can protect the worksheet against alterations, so that data is entered only in certain areas.

The **Tools** menu contains an option to protect the entire sheet against change. Before choosing this option, you must identify those areas of the sheet where changes are to be allowed. Users of the sheet will then not be able to overwrite data accidentally.

If you apply a password, users will have to enter the correct password before any changes can be made.

Clear for unprotected cells

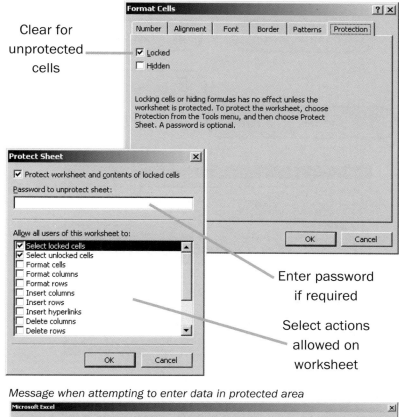

Enter password if required

Select actions allowed on worksheet

Message when attempting to enter data in protected area

Format styles

For simple sheets and one-off applications, the ability to copy formats between cells is all you need. For more complex applications, however, it is useful to give names to the format combinations you use.

A **style** is a combination of number/text format, alignment, font, border, pattern, colour and protection status. All you have to do is give the style a name, and this can be applied to any other range in the worksheet.

The use of styles is particularly important when you are creating a series of worksheets or wish to devise a company standard to be used by a number of people.

1 Apply the necessary formatting to an individual cell.

2 With the cell highlighted, select **Format > Style**.

3 Enter a new name in the **Style** box.

4 You can restrict the style to just some of the formatting features. For instance, you may set up a style for everything except the number format; all cells with this style will have the same appearance (font, alignment etc.) but can have different number formats. Clear the check boxes for those styles you don't want to include in the style.

5 If any aspect of the format is incorrect, click on the **Modify** button and make the changes.

6 Click on **OK** when the style is complete or **Cancel** to abandon.

The new style can now be applied to other cells or ranges.

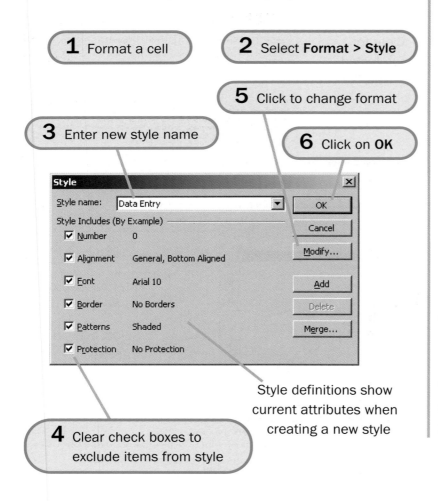

1 Format a cell

2 Select **Format > Style**

5 Click to change format

3 Enter new style name

6 Click on **OK**

4 Clear check boxes to exclude items from style

Style definitions show current attributes when creating a new style

When a style has been defined, you can use it as follows:

◆ To apply a style to a range of cells, highlight the range and then click on the required style from the **Style** box in the **Format > Style** window. Any existing formatting on the cells is lost.

◆ After applying a style, individual formatting elements can be overridden for selected cells (for instance, you can change the colour of a cell but the other style elements stay the same).

◆ To change a style, select **Format > Style**, choose the style from the drop-down list and click on **Modify**. Then update any element of the style. When you click on **OK**, all cells that have this style are updated (except where the style has been overridden by manual changes).

◆ To delete a style, select **Format > Style**, choose the style and click on **Delete**. Any cells with this style have the style removed (effectively, they are given the **Normal** style) but any later formatting that was added manually still applies.

◆ To use styles from other worksheets, select **Format > Style** and click on **Merge**.

Style box added to **Formatting** toolbar

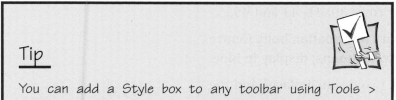

Click to select existing style

Exercises

1   Open the Timesheet.xls sheet from Chapter 4. Change the title in A1 to 14-point bold, blue text and centre it across columns A to H.

	A	B	C	D	E	F	G	H	I	J
1				**Monthly Timesheet**					2006	
2										
3	Name:	J Smith								
4	Month:	May								
5										
6					Hours				Expenses	
7	Date		Project 1	Project 2	Project 3	Project 4	TOTAL	Details	Amount	
35	Sun	28					0			
36	Mon	29					0			
37	Tue	30	3	4		1	8			
38	Wed	31					0			
39	Total		66	39	24	19	148		24.35	
40										
41				SUMMARY		Hours	148.00			
42						x Rate	7.00			
43						Pay	1036.00			
44						Expenses	24.35			
45						Total Due	£1,060.35			
46										

2   Make the year 12-point bold and blue, and make the text in A3:B4 bold and blue.

3   Make the titles in rows 6 and 7 bold and right-align the text where appropriate. Centre the 'Hours' and 'Expenses' titles over the relevant columns.

4   Increase the row height for rows 39, 41, 43 and 45.

5   Make the totals and summary information bold. Centre the 'SUMMARY' text over two columns; display in blue.

6   Give all monetary amounts two decimal places and the Total Due a currency symbol.

7   Apply border lines to the totals as shown.

8   Apply background shading to the totals, as illustrated.

9   Create formulae to show the day of the week in column A. (Hint: Start by creating a hidden column of dates.)

6 Workbooks

Multiple worksheets

So far, we have considered just a single worksheet. However, Excel allows you to have several worksheets in a single file, which is referred to as a **workbook**. A workbook may also contain chart sheets, where you can display graphs and charts of the data from your worksheets.

Whenever you save the file, **all** sheets in the workbook will be saved together. Similarly, loading a file loads into memory **all** the sheets in the workbook.

The sheets are shown in the sheet tabs at the bottom of the window.

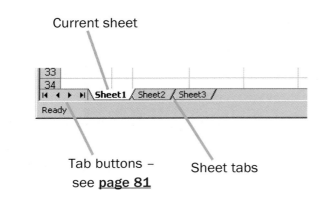

Current sheet

Tab buttons –
see **page 81**

Sheet tabs

The sheets in a workbook can be of two different types:

- **Worksheets**, for the entry of data and formulae and the calculation of results

- **Chart sheets**, for the display of graphs and charts (see **page 98**).

Take note

Previous versions of Excel allowed Visual Basic sheets and Dialog sheets. These are now accessed with the Visual Basic Editor – see *page 112*.

*Pop-up menu
for worksheets*

| Insert... |
| Delete |
| Rename |
| Move or Copy... |
| Select All Sheets |
| Tab Color... |
| View Code |

To display the pop-up menu, right-click on the sheet tab that is to be changed

Tip

Only include worksheets in a workbook if there is going to be some beneficial effect from doing so. For instance, if data from one sheet is used on another sheet or a series of sheets are always printed together in a report, then it is worth putting them all in the same workbook.

However, if a number of worksheets are similar but not related in any other way, they are probably better saved in separate files; otherwise you are just making matters unnecessarily complicated.

Basic steps

- **To rename a sheet in a workbook:**

1 Double-click on the sheet tab at the bottom of the window.

2 Enter a new name in the sheet tab; the name can use any characters (maximum length 31), including spaces.

3 Press [**Enter**]. The new name is shown in the sheet tab, which expands to show the full name.

You can also rename sheets with **Format > Sheet > Rename**.

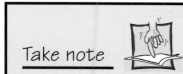

Don't confuse the sheet name in the sheet tab with the workbook name (shown in the window's title bar).

The name in the sheet tab is the name by which a particular worksheet is identified.

The workbook name is the filename under which the set of sheets is saved.

Each sheet in the workbook has a tab at the bottom of the window. Initially the sheets are called Sheet1, Sheet2, etc. but these names can be changed to something more meaningful.

By default, Excel gives you three sheets for each workbook but this number can be increased when necessary – see **page 82**.

'Sheet1' renamed as 'Summary'

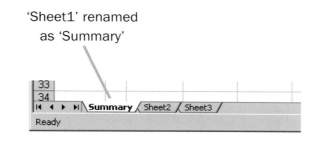

The **View** tab for **Tools > Options** changes the way in which worksheets are displayed. Some of these features relate to the current worksheet only; others affect the whole workbook.

Options for whole workbook

Current worksheet only

Starting a new sheet

To start a new worksheet in the workbook, simply click on any of the sheet tabs at the bottom of the window: for example, Sheet2. You will be presented with a completely blank sheet, in which a new set of data, formulae and titles can be entered.

This sheet need have no connection with any other sheet in the workbook, other than the fact that all sheets are saved and loaded together.

1 Click on a new sheet tab to display a blank worksheet.

2 Double-click on the sheet tab to change the sheet name. (Alternatively, right-click on the sheet tab and select **Rename**.) Edit the name in the sheet tab or type a new name for the sheet.

3 Start entering data and formulae, then save the workbook.

When you run out of blank sheets, you can insert a new one – see **page 82**. You can also change the order of the sheets.

'Sheet1' renamed as 'Summary' 'Sheet2' renamed as '1st Quarter'

1 Click on sheet tab

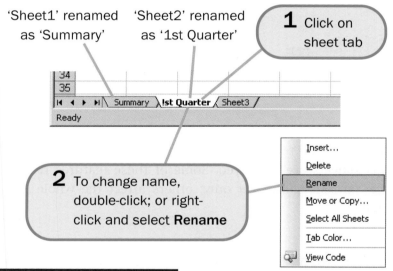

2 To change name, double-click; or right-click and select **Rename**

Tip

If there are many sheets in the workbook, it may be worth putting a menu sheet at the front of the workbook with work-sheets selected by clicking on buttons – see page 113.

Take note

If you make a major mistake in a sheet (for example, deleting the wrong range of cells), you should undo the error with [Ctrl]+[Z] immediately. Alternatively, close and re-open the file, restoring the file to the state it was in when you last saved it. Otherwise, if you move to another sheet in the same file, make changes and save the file, your mistakes in the first sheet will also be saved.

Tab buttons

The four tab buttons work as follows:

- The first button displays the first sheet tab.

- The second button displays the tab on the left of the visible tabs.

- The third button displays the tab on the right of the visible tabs.

- The fourth button displays the last sheet tab in the workbook.

You can switch from one sheet to another simply by clicking on the sheet tabs at the bottom of the window. When a tab is clicked, the corresponding sheet is displayed in the window and the sheet name is highlighted on the tab.

When you have a number of sheets, you will not be able to see all the tabs. The tabs can be scrolled to the left or right with the small tab buttons. Clicking on these buttons determines which tabs are displayed; they do not select a different sheet.

The bar along the bottom is shared by the sheet tabs and the horizontal scroll bars. You can change the amount used for each by dragging the divider to the left or right.

Show first tab   Show previous tab   Drag to change share of bar

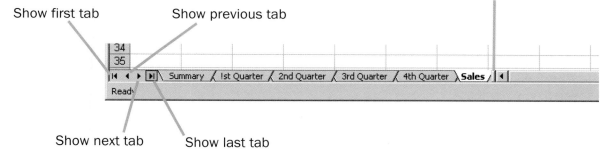

Show next tab   Show last tab

Take note

When you select a different sheet, any changes you have made to the other sheets are not lost; the data is still held in memory. When you save the workbook, the contents of all sheets are saved.

Tip

Include the sheet name in a title cell, so that you can always see at a glance which sheet you are working on (particularly when the workbook contains several similar sheets). Otherwise, the sheet tab may be the only way of identifying the current sheet, and this is not included when the file is printed.

Changing worksheets

You are free to insert new sheets, copy sheets, change the order of sheets and delete unwanted sheets.

To insert a new sheet, click on one of the sheet tabs and then select **Insert > Worksheet** to add a new worksheet. The worksheet is inserted to the left of the selected sheet and becomes the active sheet. To add a new chart sheet, use **Insert > Chart** (see **page 88** for details of charts).

You can add several worksheets at once by selecting the corresponding number of existing sheet tabs. For example, to insert three new sheets, first select a group of three existing tabs.

To delete an unwanted sheet, click on the sheet tab and then select **Edit > Delete Sheet**. (Always save the workbook first, in case you make a mistake – you cannot undo a worksheet deletion.)

Insert options

New sheets are inserted as follows:

- By selecting the **Insert > Worksheet** option to add a new worksheet or **Insert > Chart** to add a new chart.

- By clicking on the **As New Sheet** button in the final step when defining a chart (see **page 93**).

Charts on normal worksheets can also be converted to separate chart sheets (see **page 98**).

Number of sheets shown on sheet tab when new workbook is started

Select this option to display the Properties dialog box whenever a workbook is saved with a new name (see **page 8**)

Take note

The General tab for Tools > Options affects the overall operation of Excel. These options apply to all your workbooks, not just the current one.

Options ?|x|

| Color | International | Save | Error Checking | Spelling | Security |
| View | Calculation | Edit | General | Transition | Custom Lists | Chart |

Settings

☐ R1C1 reference style
☐ Ignore other applications
☑ Function tooltips
☑ Recently used file list: 4 entries

☐ Prompt for workbook properties
☐ Provide feedback with sound
☐ Zoom on roll with IntelliMouse

Web Options... | Service Options...

Sheets in new workbook: 3
Standard font: Arial | Size: 10
Default file location: C:\
At startup, open all files in:
User name: Stephen Morris

OK | Cancel

To move a sheet to a different position in the workbook, click on the sheet tab and then drag it across the tabs to its new position.

To make a copy of a sheet in the same workbook, click on the sheet tab, press and hold **[Ctrl]**, and then drag the tab to the point at which you want to insert the copy sheet.

You can move or copy a number of sheets if you start by marking a group of tabs.

You can display more than one sheet at a time using **Window > New Window**. Use **Window > Arrange** to organise the display.

The example below shows a workbook with two worksheets displayed. The sheets have been resized and repositioned.

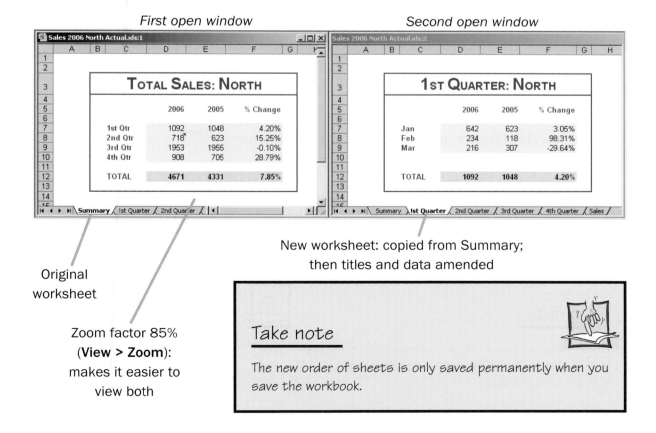

First open window

Second open window

Sales 2006 North Actual.xls:1

	A	B	C	D	E	F	G	H
1								
2								
3		**TOTAL SALES: NORTH**						
4								
5				2006	2005	% Change		
6								
7			1st Qtr	1092	1048	4.20%		
8			2nd Qtr	718	623	15.25%		
9			3rd Qtr	1953	1955	-0.10%		
10			4th Qtr	908	705	28.79%		
11								
12			TOTAL	4671	4331	7.85%		
13								
14								

Summary / 1st Quarter / 2nd Quarter /

Sales 2006 North Actual.xls:2

	A	B	C	D	E	F	G	H
1								
2								
3		**1ST QUARTER: NORTH**						
4								
5				2006	2005	% Change		
6								
7			Jan	642	623	3.05%		
8			Feb	234	118	98.31%		
9			Mar	216	307	-29.64%		
10								
11								
12			TOTAL	1092	1048	4.20%		
13								
14								

Summary \ 1st Quarter / 2nd Quarter / 3rd Quarter / 4th Quarter / Sales /

New worksheet: copied from Summary; then titles and data amended

Original worksheet

Zoom factor 85% (**View > Zoom**): makes it easier to view both

Formulae in workbooks

A formula can refer to cells and ranges in other sheets in the workbook, or even a three-dimensional range covering several worksheets.

To reference a cell in another sheet, precede the cell reference with the sheet name and an exclamation mark. For instance, the summary sheet in the Sales example will include the total value from cell D12 in the 1st Quarter worksheet if cell D7 contains the formula:

='1st Quarter'!D12

The single quotes are needed to avoid confusion in this instance, because of the space in the sheet name. If there are no spaces in the worksheet name, you do not need to use quotes.

When this formula is copied to other cells, it is updated like any other relative reference (e.g. the value in E7 is '1st Quarter'!E12).

A formula may also refer to a range in another sheet:

=SUM('1st Quarter'!D7:D9)

This formula adds the contents of all cells in the range D7:D9 in the 1st Quarter sheet, putting the answer in the selected cell of the current sheet.

Basic steps

■ **To enter the total in D7 of the Summary sheet:**

1 Display two windows for the workbook, one showing the Summary sheet, the other the 1st Quarter sheet.

2 Click on D7 in the Summary sheet.

3 Type = in the cell.

4 Click on the 1st Quarter sheet and then on cell D12; the formula is updated as you do so.

5 Press [**Enter**].

Any change in D7, D8 or D9 in the 1st Quarter sheet results in a corresponding change in D7 in the Summary sheet.

Take note

If you need to use quotes in sheet references use ordinary single quotes. Don't try to insert 'smart quotes'; Excel will not recognise these.

Tip

If you insert or delete rows and columns in one sheet, the formulae in other sheets are updated accordingly. Treat the workbook as one large grid, spread over several sheets.

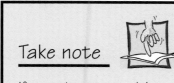
A formula can refer to a three-dimensional block of cells that covers two or more consecutive sheets. The range of sheets is placed before the exclamation mark, the range of cells after it.

For example, the grand total of sales in the Summary sheet could just as well have been calculated by:

=SUM('1st Quarter:4th Quarter'!D7:D9)

This will add the contents of all cells in the range D7:D9 in all sheets from 1st Quarter to 4th Quarter. In three-dimensional references, the same range of cells is used in all sheets. If you think of the sheets as lying one above another, this effectively gives you a three-dimensional rectangular block of cells.

If a sheet name uses characters other than numbers and letters (e.g. 1st Quarter), any sheet reference must be enclosed in single quotes. The quotes are not needed for single-word names that contain only numbers and letters (e.g. Summary, Sheet1). For ranges of sheets, a single pair of quotes encloses both sheet names (as in '1st Quarter:4th Quarter').

You can also link to cells in another workbook. Open two workbooks and create the formula in the same way as for linking across two worksheets. The formula will include the workbook name in square brackets; for example:

='[Area51.xls]Totals'!$E$9

This is an absolute reference to cell E9 on the Totals sheet of the workbook in Area51.xls.

When you load a file that has formulae which refer to cells in other workbooks, you are given the opportunity to update the values in the workbook with the current values from the referenced sheets (even if those files are not currently open). If the referenced file can't be found, you are given the option to leave the worksheet as it is or edit the links to the other workbook.

Exercises

1 Open the Timesheet.xls file from Chapter 5. Rename the worksheet with the month name.

2 Copy the contents of the sheet to two further sheets and amend them to hold data for two other months.

3 Insert a new Summary sheet, positioning it to the left of the existing sheets.

4 Set up the Summary sheet so that it can display the totals from the individual monthly sheets. Apply appropriate formatting.

	A	B	C	D	E	F	G	H	I	J	K
1		**Timesheet Summary**						2006			
2											
3	Name:	J Smith									
4											
5											
6					Hours				Expenses	TOTAL	
7		Month		Project 1	Project 2	Project 3	Project 4	TOTAL	PAY	Amount	DUE
8											
9		Apr		44	35	35	30	144	1008.00	35.34	1043.34
10		May		66	39	24	19	148	1036.00	24.35	1060.35
11		Jun		52	33	46	17	148	1036.00	17.22	1053.22
12											
13		Total		162	107	105	66	440	3080.00	76.91	3156.91
14											
15											

5 Add formulae that copy the totals from each of the monthly sheets into the ranges C9:F11 and H9:I11. Add formulae to calculate the other totals.

6 Change the data in the original sheets. Check that the copied totals match the totals in the original sheets and that the totals in columns I and J of the Summary sheet match those in the original sheets.

7 Charts and graphs

Chart Wizard

Excel provides a wide range of options for displaying any set of data as a chart or graph: bar charts, pie charts, line graphs and others. The chart can be placed anywhere on the worksheet and can be made to fit a rectangle of any size or shape. Once it has been created, any aspects of the chart can be changed. Alternatively, you can create a separate chart sheet.

A chart is created on the worksheet using the Chart Wizard, which provides you with a series of dialog boxes that are used to build up the display.

Before starting the Chart Wizard, you should mark the block of data to be charted.

1 Mark the range of data for which the chart is to be created. Include the row of labels above the data and the column to the left, if appropriate.

2 Click on the **Chart Wizard** button. The first of four dialog boxes is displayed.

(If the button is not visible on the toolbar, click on the drop-down button at the end of the toolbar and then on the **Chart Wizard** button.)

1 Mark data area

TOTAL SALES: NORTH

	2006	2005	% Change
1st Qtr	1092	1048	4.20%
2nd Qtr	718	623	15.25%
3rd Qtr	1953	1955	-0.10%
4th Qtr	908	705	28.79%
TOTAL	4671	4331	7.85%

2 Click on Chart Wizard

More buttons

100%

Chart Wizard

Drawing toolbar

Zoom factor

Excel Help

Include row and column headings – these will be shown on the axes of the completed graph

Take note

You can include blank rows and columns in the range – these will be ignored. The range can be made up of non-adjacent blocks, if the data comes from different parts of the sheet.

Chart type

3 Click on a chart type. The default is the **Column** chart but there are 13 others. The dialog box shows several variations of the selected type.

4 Click on a sub-type and then on **Next**.

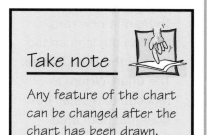

Take note

Any feature of the chart can be changed after the chart has been drawn.

The Chart Wizard offers 14 different types of chart. These fall into three broad categories:

◆ **Bar charts** have a rectangular bar for each item of data, the height of the bar being proportional to the data value.

◆ **Graphs** plot a series of points, with each point being determined by a pair of co-ordinates. Usually, consecutive points are joined together by a line.

◆ **Pie charts** consist of a circle divided into segments. The values in the data series are totalled, so that each value can be calculated as a percentage of the total. The sizes of the segments are proportional to these percentages.

The options provided are variations on these: for instance, three-dimensional bars or area graphs (where the value is represented by the area under the graph).

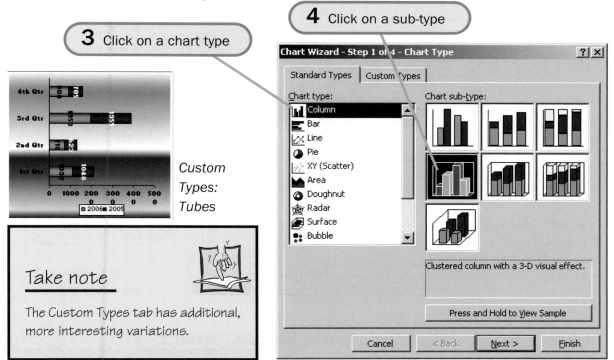

Custom Types: Tubes

Take note

The Custom Types tab has additional, more interesting variations.

Data range

The data range consists of one or more rows or columns; each row or column will provide the data for one series of bars or for one line on a line graph.

You can choose either rows or columns for the data series. If you choose **rows**, the data values in each row form one set of bars or the points on one line; the column headings are the labels for the chart. If you choose **columns**, each column is a data series and the row headings are used as chart labels.

5 The second dialog box gives you the opportunity to change the data range that has been selected. You either mark the range by dragging the pointer on the worksheet or edit the range in the dialog box.

To mark a new range, click on the icon on the right of the **Data Range**. The Chart Wizard is reduced to a small box. Mark the data area (including labels), then click on the icon on the right of the reduced dialog box.

6 Select either rows or columns as the basis for the data series.

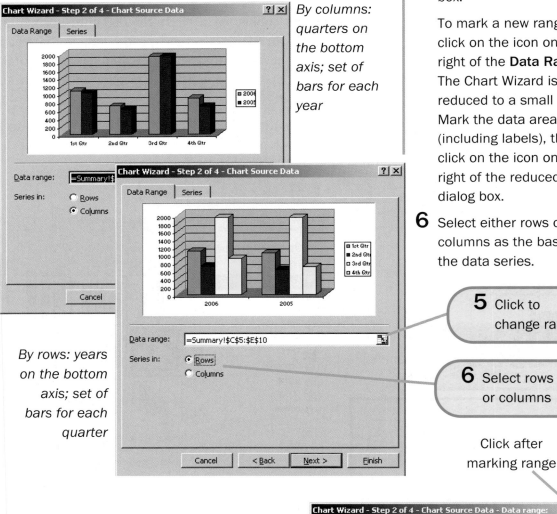

By columns: quarters on the bottom axis; set of bars for each year

By rows: years on the bottom axis; set of bars for each quarter

5 Click to change range

6 Select rows or columns

Click after marking range

Series

7 Click on the **Series** tab and change the ranges that identify the series names, values and X-axis labels. Click on **Next** when the ranges are correct.

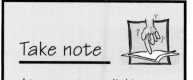

Take note

At any step, clicking on Back takes you back to the previous step, where you can make further changes.

Within the marked range, you should have a block of data and the labels that will be shown on the graph. The **Series** tab for Step 2 lets you change these ranges.

There will be one graph or one set of bars for each series. For each of these series you can identify a range containing the series name (e.g. the year) and a range of values.

The range for the **X-axis labels** defines the cells whose contents will be printed along the bottom of the chart.

You can change any range by clicking on the icon to the right of the entry box.

Current settings for '2006' series:

Series name (D5:D6)	2006
Values (D7:D10)	1092 to 908
Category labels (C7:C10)	1st Qtr to 4th Qtr

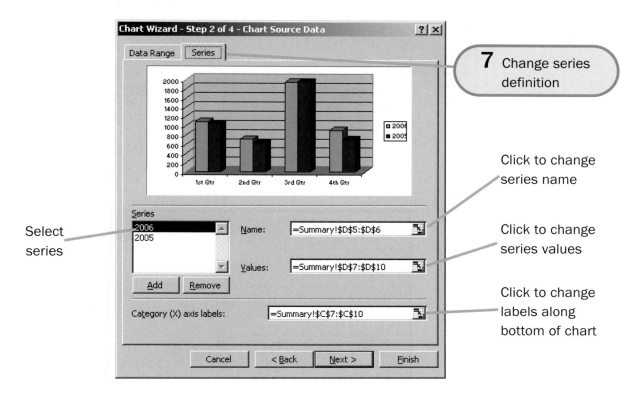

Select series

7 Change series definition

Click to change series name

Click to change series values

Click to change labels along bottom of chart

Titles and labels

The third dialog box lets you add explanatory text to the chart. The chart title is printed above the graph, and the axis titles are added alongside the axis labels. Other tabs let you alter further features of the chart. For example, the legend is a box showing the colours or types of points used for each data series.

8 Enter some text for the chart title and for each of the axes. Make any further changes with the other tabs, then click on **Next**.

8 Enter titles and axis labels

Chart title

Z-axis (value) label

Legend

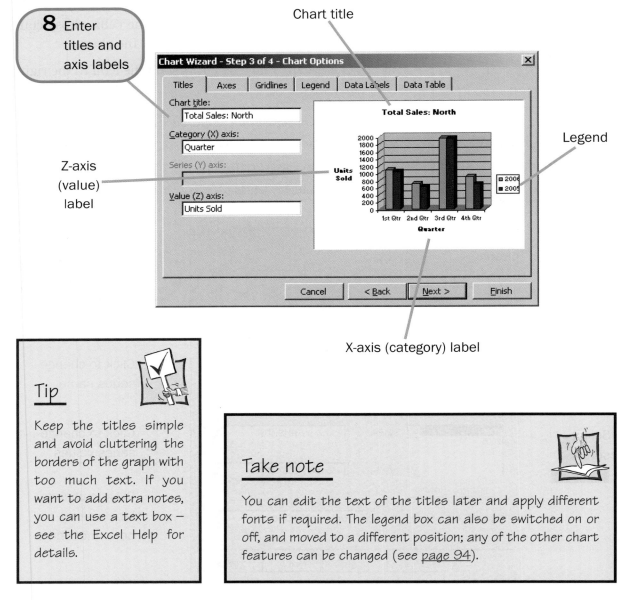

X-axis (category) label

Location

9 Choose the location for the chart: a separate sheet or an existing worksheet.

Click on **Finish**. The new chart will be displayed and can be edited if necessary.

The final dialog box gives you the choice between overlaying the new chart on one of the worksheets (**As Object In**) or placing it in a new sheet (**As New Sheet**).

If you choose to keep the chart on an existing worksheet, you can select a sheet from the drop-down list. When the chart has been added you can move it around and resize it, as required.

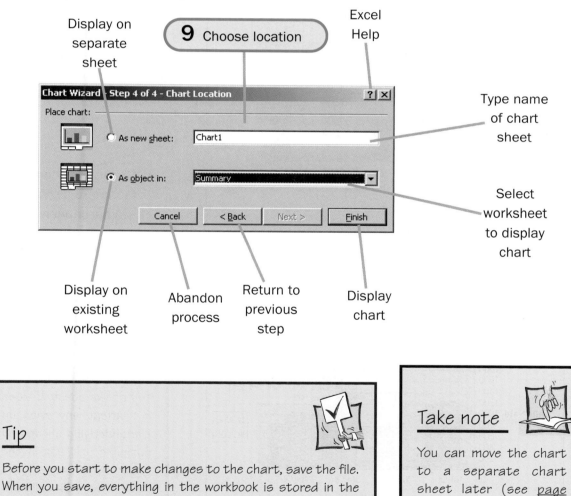

Display on separate sheet

9 Choose location

Excel Help

Type name of chart sheet

Select worksheet to display chart

Display on existing worksheet

Abandon process

Return to previous step

Display chart

Tip

Before you start to make changes to the chart, save the file. When you save, everything in the workbook is stored in the file, including the chart set-up.

Take note

You can move the chart to a separate chart sheet later (see page 98).

Editing the chart

When the chart has been drawn, it can be moved to a new position on the sheet and can be resized to fit any reasonable gap.

If you place the mouse pointer over any part of the chart, a descriptive label pops up. If you point to a data item, the label shows you the series name and data value.

- ■ To move the chart, click on it and then drag it to a new position.

- ■ To change the size, click on the chart and then drag the sizing handles on the corners and sides. Hold down [**Shift**] while you drag to keep the proportions the same.

- ■ To remove a chart from a sheet, click on the chart and press [**Delete**].

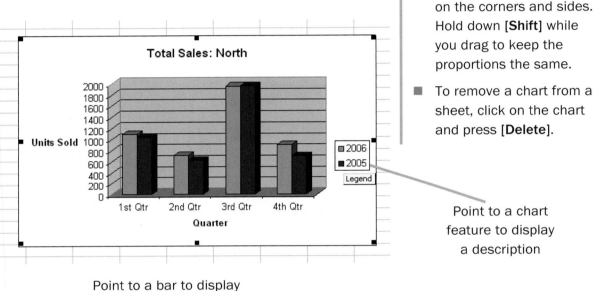

Point to a chart feature to display a description

Point to a bar to display series name and data value

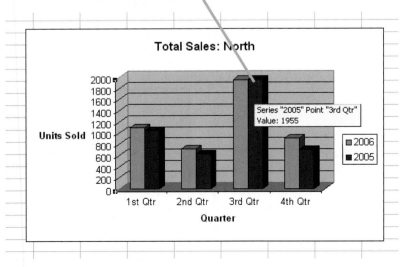

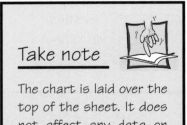
94

Basic steps

1 Double-click on any item on the chart: text, labels, grid lines, grid background, legend, bars or lines, etc.

2 In the dialog box that appears, make any changes that are needed to the appearance of the chart and then click on **OK**.

So far the chart has been produced using a limited number of options. You are now free to change any aspect of the chart: colours, fonts, patterns, line styles and so on.

Format Chart Area

| Patterns | Font | Properties |

Border
- ◉ Automatic
- ○ None
- ○ Custom

Style: _____
Color: Automatic
Weight: _____

☐ Shadow
☐ Round corners

Sample

Area
- ◉ Automatic
- ○ None

Fill Effects...

OK   Cancel

Options for chart area (chart background, font and general properties)

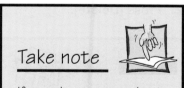
Options for axes

Format Axis

| Patterns | Scale | Font | Number | Alignment |

Font: Arial
- Algerian
- Anna
- Antique Olive
- Arial

Font style: Regular
- Regular
- Italic
- Bold
- Bold Italic

Size: 10
- 8
- 9
- 10
- 11

Underline: None
Color: Automatic
Background: Automatic

Effects
- ☐ Strikethrough
- ☐ Superscript
- ☐ Subscript

Preview

AaBbCcYyZz

☑ Auto scale

This is a TrueType font. The same font will be used on both your printer and your screen.

OK   Cancel

The **Chart** toolbar provides options for making quick changes to certain aspects of the chart.

Chart

Chart Area

95

Changing chart data

You can change the range of data displayed on the chart at any time.

- ◆ New rows or columns can be added, increasing the scope of the chart.

- ◆ The range can be extended or contracted to show more or less data.

- ◆ The range can be changed completely, so that it covers a different set of data.

- ◆ Data series can be removed from the chart.

All of these tasks can be accomplished by clicking on the chart and then selecting the **Chart** > **Source Data** menu option and the **Series** tab. You can change the ranges for any of the series, or click on **Add** to add a new series or **Remove** to delete a series from the chart. There are also alternative methods for making some of these changes.

Alternatives

- ■ **To add a new series or extend an existing series:**

1 Mark the new range (including labels).

2 Click on the range border (the pointer changes shape) and drag it into the chart.

3 Unless it is obvious to Excel how the data is to be displayed, you will be asked to fill in a **Paste Special** dialog box.

4 The chart is extended to show the new data.

- ■ **To delete a data series:**

1 Click on one of the bars or data points.

2 Press [**Delete**].

Choose between new series and extra points for existing series

Select direction of data series (either in rows or columns)

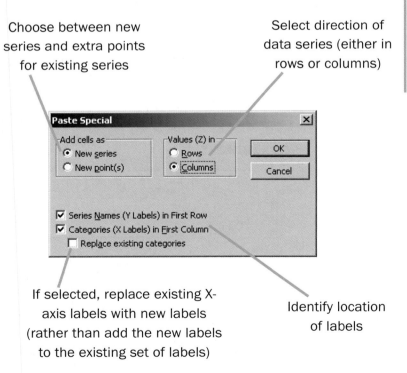

If selected, replace existing X-axis labels with new labels (rather than add the new labels to the existing set of labels)

Identify location of labels

Tip

Always save the work-sheet before dragging new ranges to the chart — the results are not always what you expect. You can usually undo the changes with [Ctrl]+[Z] but it is safer to save first.

- **To change the view for a 3-D chart:**

1 Click on the chart to select it.

2 Select **3-D View** from the **Chart** menu.

3 To rotate the chart vertically, click on the buttons to the left of the chart.

4 To rotate the chart horizontally, click on one of the buttons below the chart.

5 Click on **Apply** to see the effect of the current settings.

6 Click on **OK** to finish.

When a chart has been selected by clicking on it, some of the menus at the top of the window change. For instance, the options are reduced in the Insert and View menus; the Format menu provides a new range of options for changing the way in which the chart is displayed.

There is also a new **Chart** menu, replacing the **Data** menu. The first four options in the full menu correspond to the four steps in the Chart Wizard, and bring up the same dialog boxes.

The **Chart > Add Data** option adds in another data series.

The **Chart > Add Trendline** option performs regression analysis on a bar chart or graph, allowing you to predict future values by extending the trend line beyond the actual data.

The **Chart > 3-D View** option allows you to rotate a three-dimensional chart, both horizontally and vertically.

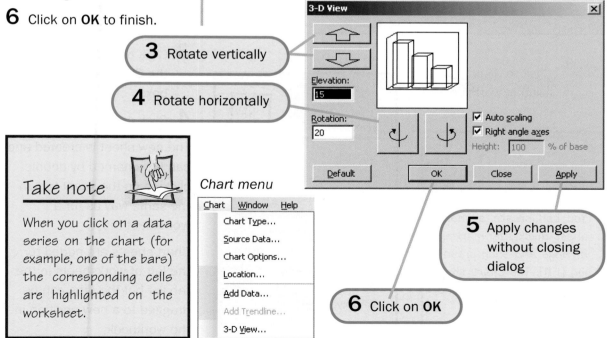

3 Rotate vertically

4 Rotate horizontally

5 Apply changes without closing dialog

6 Click on **OK**

Chart menu

Take note

When you click on a data series on the chart (for example, one of the bars) the corresponding cells are highlighted on the worksheet.

Chart sheets

Much of the time you will include charts as part of a normal worksheet. However, you may want to use a chart as a transparency for an overhead projector, as a handout during a presentation, or simply as an individual page in a report. In these cases, you can create a separate chart sheet within the workbook.

The chart sheet can be created from scratch or derived from an existing chart on a worksheet.

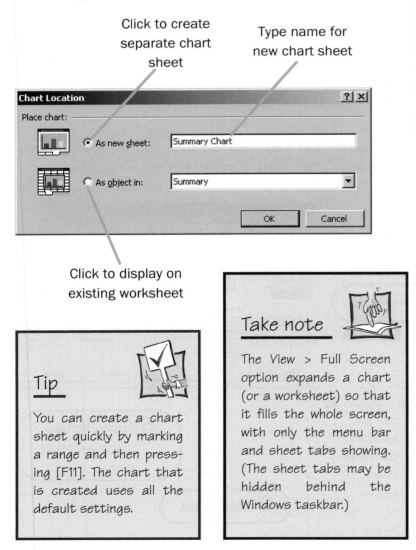

Click to create separate chart sheet

Type name for new chart sheet

Click to display on existing worksheet

Basic steps

- **To create a chart sheet:**

1 Mark the range to be charted.

2 Select **Chart** from the **Insert** menu.

3 Complete the Chart Wizard dialog boxes, as before. In the final step, select **As new sheet**.

The result is that a new sheet is created (this time, a chart sheet), with a default name of **Chart1**.

- **To convert a worksheet into a chart sheet:**

1 Click on the chart.

2 Select **Location** from the **Chart** menu.

3 Click on **As new sheet** in the **Chart Location** dialog box.

4 Click on **OK**.

The new sheet is created and can be renamed by double-clicking on the sheet tab, in the same way as for a worksheet tab.

Chart sheets are added to the left of worksheets in the tab list but the tabs can be dragged to a new position in the workbook.

Tip

You can create a chart sheet quickly by marking a range and then pressing [F11]. The chart that is created uses all the default settings.

Take note

The View > Full Screen option expands a chart (or a worksheet) so that it fills the whole screen, with only the menu bar and sheet tabs showing. (The sheet tabs may be hidden behind the Windows taskbar.)

Options

- Rename the sheet by double-clicking on the sheet tab.

- Change the position of the sheet in the workbook by dragging the sheet tab to a new position.

- Delete the chart sheet by selecting it and then choosing **Delete Sheet** from the **Edit** menu. Alternatively, right-click on the sheet tab and select **Delete**.

The chart sheet behaves in the same way as a worksheet and is saved as part of the workbook. The chart sheet can be renamed, moved to a new position or deleted. You can also display it in a separate window or print it.

Chart sheet shown at Full Screen

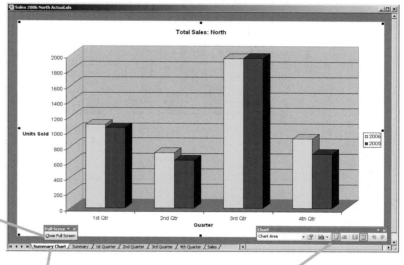

Full Screen toolbar – click button for Normal view

Chart sheet name

Chart toolbar – can be moved or closed

Tip

You can display the Chart toolbar by selecting View > Toolbars and clicking on the Chart option.

When you click on an element of the chart, the element name is shown on the left of the toolbar and its properties can be changed using the buttons on the rest of the toolbar.

Take note

You can copy a chart from a worksheet to a chart sheet. Click once on the blank area of the chart (so that the sizing handles are shown at the corners) and press [Ctrl]+[C] to copy it to the Clipboard; then open the chart sheet and press [Ctrl]+[V] to paste in the chart.

Similarly, you can copy a chart from a chart sheet onto a worksheet. In this case you must click in the white area outside the chart, so that the sizing handles are shown on the corners of the chart sheet.

99

Exercises

1   Open the Timesheet.xls file from Chapter 6. Create a chart based on the range A7:F11, showing the total time spent on each project.

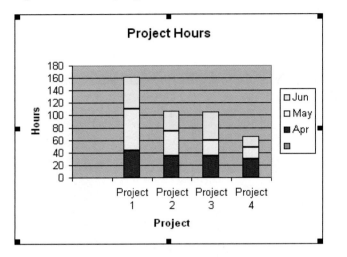

2   Edit the chart so that the blank row and column are excluded.

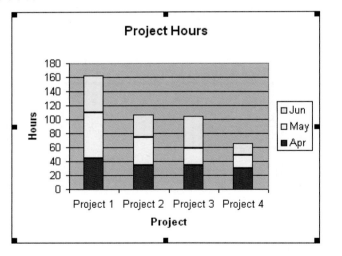

3   Copy the chart to a separate chart sheet and save the workbook.

8 Printing

Page set-up

The Page Setup option in the Excel **File** menu lets you determine the way in which a particular sheet will be printed. There are four tabs, the first of which contains the **Page** settings:

◆ **Orientation** gives you either portrait (tall, thin) pages or landscape (pages printed sideways).

◆ **Scaling** is either a fixed percentage (e.g. 50% to reduce everything to half size) or the largest size possible for the sheets to fit the page. For best-fit scaling, choose the number of pages to be printed.

◆ **Paper size** provides a range of standard page sizes.

◆ **Print quality** (the resolution in terms of dots per inch) is available only for some types of printer.

◆ **First page number** determines the page number for the first page; if the setting is **Auto** the page number defaults to 1, unless this print run follows on from another, in which case page numbering carries on from the previous run.

Basic steps

To display the **Page** settings for the current workbook:

1 In Excel, select **Page Setup** from the **File** menu.

2 Click on the **Page** tab (if necessary).

3 Select the required options.

The page settings apply to the current worksheet only. Therefore you can have different settings for each sheet.

Tip

On laser printers, there is a certain margin on each edge where nothing can be printed. Make sure your margin settings are large enough to include this area (see opposite).

Page Setup   ? ×

| Page | Margins | Header/Footer | Sheet |

Orientation

[A] ⦿ Portrait   [A] ○ Landscape

Print...

Print Preview

Options...

Scaling

⦿ Adjust to: [100] ⬆⬇ % normal size

○ Fit to: [1] ⬆⬇ page(s) wide by [1] ⬆⬇ tall

Paper size: [A4 (210 x 297 mm) ▼]

Print quality: [600 dpi ▼]

First page number: [Auto]

OK   Cancel

Start printing

See what the page will look like when printed

Printer options (specific to selected printer type)

Options

- The **Top** margin is the space above the main text area, including the space used by the header.

- The **Bottom** margin is the space below the text area, including any footer.

- The **Left** and **Right** margins are the spaces on either side.

- The **Header** and **Footer** settings determine the positions of the header and footer within the top and bottom margins (being the distance from the edge of the paper).

- The **Center on Page** options let you centre any sheet that does not fill the page. The sheet can be centred horizontally, vertically or both.

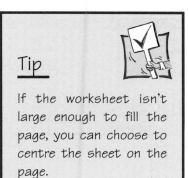

Tip

If the worksheet isn't large enough to fill the page, you can choose to centre the sheet on the page.

Margins

The **Margins** tab on the **Page Setup** box lets you decide how much blank space there should be at the top, bottom and sides of the sheet.

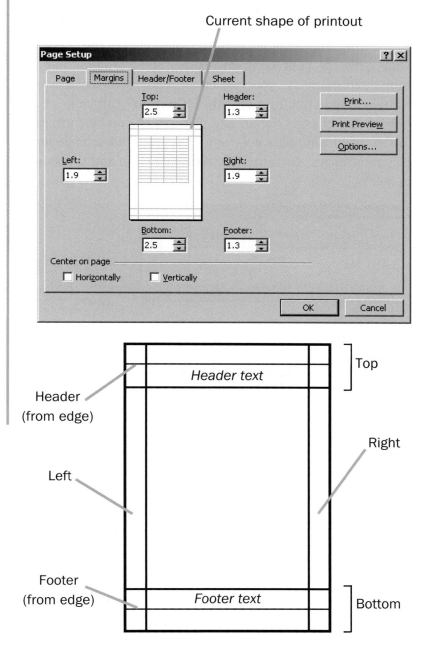

Headers and footers

You can choose a piece of text to be printed at the top and bottom of every page. The header and footer can cover several lines and each has three sections: for printing on the left, right or centre of the page.

A standard header/footer can be selected from the list, which offers defaults such as the sheet name, the filename, your name or your company name, and various combinations. Alternatively, you can create your own headers and footers by clicking on the **Custom** buttons. Each header/footer can contain any text (which can be formatted in the usual way) plus a variety of special codes: page number, total pages, current date, time, filename and worksheet name.

- The **Header** is a piece of text that is printed at the top of each page.

- The **Footer** is text that appears at the bottom of every page.

#	Page number
	Total pages
	Current date
	Current time
	Path/filename
	Filename
	Worksheet tab name

Buttons for special codes   Insert picture

Format picture

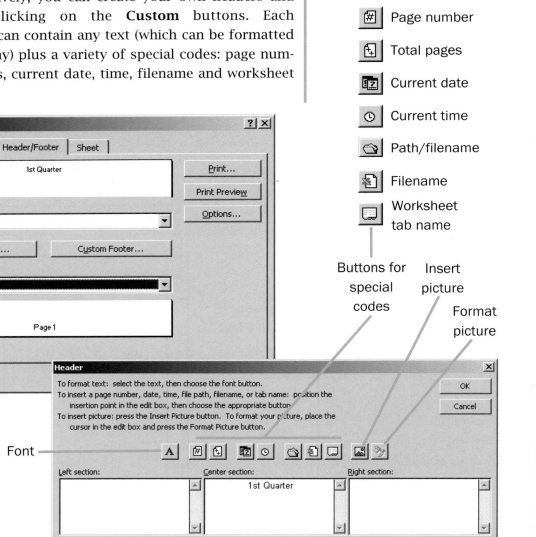

Click to customise header

Font

Options

- The **Print Area** is the default range to be printed. This is the range that will always be printed unless you specify otherwise. If you leave this box blank, the whole sheet is printed.

- The **Print Titles** are rows and columns that are to be repeated on every page when the worksheet will not fit on one page.

- The **Print** options decide which optional features will be printed, including the grid lines, row numbers and column letters. You can also select the print colours and quality. The boxes on the right let you choose whether to print comments (and if so, where) and the way in which any errors will be represented.

- The **Page Order** is used when the worksheet is both too long and too wide for one page; this option decides whether printing is done from top to bottom and then left to right, or vice versa.

Sheet settings

The final **Page Setup** tab determines the way in which the sheet itself is printed.

You can select the ranges for the **Print Area** and **Print Titles** by clicking on the icons on the right of the text boxes.

Click to select a

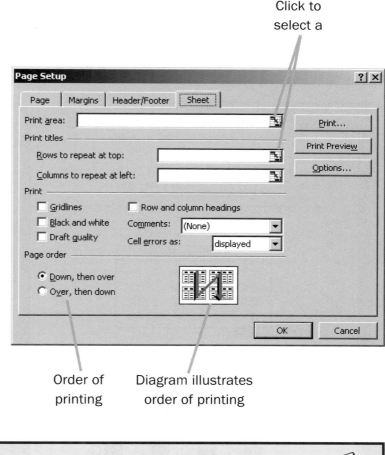

Order of printing

Diagram illustrates order of printing

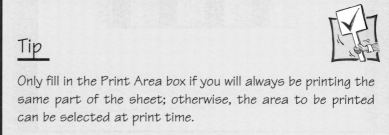

Tip

Only fill in the Print Area box if you will always be printing the same part of the sheet; otherwise, the area to be printed can be selected at print time.

Preview

The **Print Preview** option in the **File** menu lets you see on screen what the final printed page will look like. As well as zooming into or out of the display, there are options to take you directly to other printer activities (as a shortcut to the **File** menu).

Page as it will appear when printed

Main title created on worksheet

Print

Print Preview

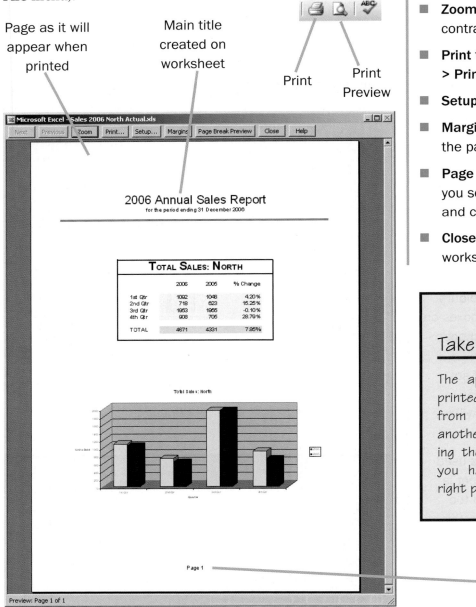

Footer

Options

- **Next** displays the next page.

- **Previous** displays the previous page.

- **Zoom** expands or contracts the display.

- **Print** takes you to the **File > Print** options.

- **Setup** loads **Page Setup**.

- **Margins** lets you change the page margins.

- **Page Break Preview** lets you see the page breaks and change them.

- **Close** returns you to the worksheet.

Take note

The appearance of the printed page may vary from one printer to another. Before previewing the page make sure you have selected the right printer.

Options

The **Print range** section lets you choose the number of pages printed. Select from:

■ **All**: the entire selection (as determined by the **Print what** box)

■ **Page(s)**: just part of the selection (specified by giving the first and last page numbers – you can see what will be printed on each page by clicking on the **Preview** button)

The information to be printed is chosen (in the **Print what** box) from:

■ **Selection**: the part of the worksheet previously marked by dragging the pointer over a range

■ **Active sheet(s)**: those sheets whose tabs are currently selected

■ **Entire workbook**: all sheets

You can also specify the number of **copies** to print. The **Collate** box gives you the choice of printing complete copies one at a time or multiple copies of each page in turn.

Print options

Once all the set-up work has been completed (and this is something you should only have to do once for each workbook), you can start printing. The **File > Print** command has a very simple dialog box although, in common with the other print commands, it has buttons to take you to other set-up stages.

Print to file for printing later or for formatting in another program

Printer properties

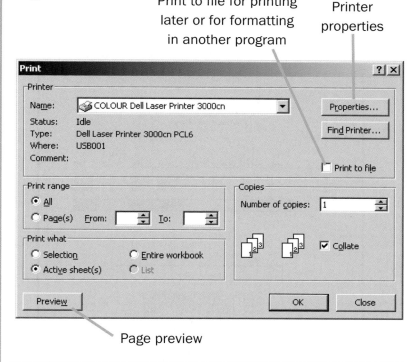

Page preview

Tip

You will not always want to print the whole sheet, so leave the Print Area blank in the Sheet settings and just mark a suitable range each time before you print. Then click on the Selection option in the Print dialog box. Remember that you can mark whole rows or columns by clicking on the row numbers or column letters. When you are ready to print the whole sheet, select the Active sheet(s) option.

Exercises

1 Open the Timesheet.xls file from Chapter 7. Set the print margins to 3cm for top and bottom and 0.9cm on left and right.

2 Add a footer, with the page number in the centre, filename on the left and date on the right.

3 Adjust the table and graph on the Summary sheet so that they are clearly visible.

4 Display the Summary sheet in **Preview** mode.

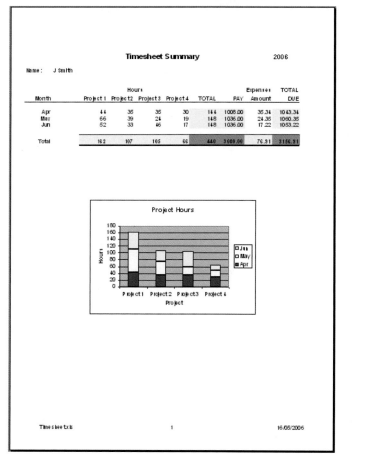

5 Print just the Summary sheet and then print the whole workbook.

9 Macros

Recording macros

A macro is a way of automating a series of frequently-used actions. At its simplest, a macro is created by recording a series of keystrokes, which can then be replayed.

When you have created a macro, you can edit it, creating a more sophisticated program. For example, you can set up the macro so that the actions taken depend on the contents of particular cells.

1 Select **Record New Macro**

2 Enter valid Excel name

Store macro in current workbook, a new workbook or your **Personal Macro Workbook** (making the macro available to all your workbooks)

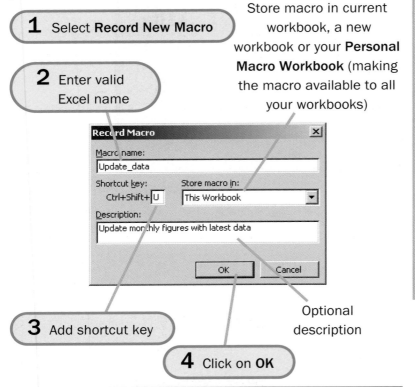

3 Add shortcut key

4 Click on **OK**

Optional description

Basic steps

1 Select **Tools > Macro** and click on **Record New Macro**.

2 Enter a name for the macro and a description. The name must be a valid Excel name (letters, numbers, underscores; no spaces).

3 If required, type a letter to be used with [**Ctrl**] as a shortcut to the macro. (You can also hold down [**Shift**] while you select the letter.)

4 Click on **OK**.

5 Any actions you now take are recorded, including any mistakes you make!

6 When you have finished, click on the **Stop** button.

5 Record actions

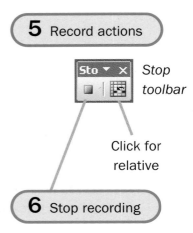

Stop toolbar

Click for relative

6 Stop recording

Take note

By default, all cell references are absolute; i.e. the same cells will be used regardless of which cell is current when the macro is run. For the macro to perform its actions relative to the start position, click on the Relative Reference button.

Macro options

The Macro box has the following buttons:

- **Run** runs the macro.

- **Cancel** returns you to the worksheet.

- **Step Into** runs the macro one step at a time, so you can see how it works and detect bugs.

- **Edit** allows you to change the macro.

- **Create** lets you write a new macro (available when you enter a new **Macro Name**).

- **Delete** permanently deletes the macro.

- **Options** lets you change the shortcut key and description.

There are several ways to run the macro:

◆ Select **Macros** from the **Tools > Macro** menu, click on the macro name and click on **Run**.

◆ If the macro was given a shortcut key, use that without selecting any menu option.

◆ Add the macro to a toolbar or menu and run it from there (see **page 112**).

You can also add a button to the worksheet and attach a macro to it (see **page 113**). Clicking on the button will then run the macro.

Take note

The macros that are available will include all macros in any open workbooks plus those in your Personal Macro Workbook.

Run the selected macro

Existing macros

Choose between all open workbooks, the current workbook and any other open workbook

Description of highlighted macro

Editing macros

Macros are written and edited in the Visual Basic programming language. When you record a macro, Excel creates a Visual Basic procedure containing the necessary code. This code can be edited and new lines can be added. The Visual Basic code is stored in a separate area of the workbook, by default named **Module1**.

To edit a macro, select **Tools** > **Macro** > **Macros**, click on the macro name and then on **Edit**.

Full details of Visual Basic procedures are given in the associated Help. From the Visual Basic **Help** menu, select **Microsoft Visual Basic Help**. (If Visual Basic Help was not included in the installation process, it can be added by re-running the **Setup** program.)

- To add a macro to a toolbar or menu:

1 Select **Tools** > **Customize**.

2 Click on the **Commands** tab and the **Macros** category.

3 Drag the **Custom Button** to a toolbar or the **Custom Menu Item** to the menu bar.

4 Click on the **Modify Selection** button in the **Customize** box and then on **Assign Macro**. Click on a macro and then on **OK**.

5 Click on **Modify Selection** again. For a custom button, use **Change Button Image** to choose a new picture. For a menu item, type a new title in the **Name** box (include **&** in front of the shortcut letter so that it is shown underlined).

6 Click on **Close**.

Clicking on the new toolbar button or menu item will now activate the macro.

```
Sales 2006 North Actual.xls - Module1 (Code)                 _|□|×|
(General)                           ▼   Save_and_Exit                    ▼

Sub Update_data()
'
' Update_data Macro
' Update monthly figures with latest data
'
' Keyboard Shortcut: Ctrl+Shift+U
'
    Range("J17:J22").Select
    Selection.Copy
    Range("L17").Select
    ActiveSheet.Paste
    Application.CutCopyMode = False
    Range("J17").Select
End Sub
Sub Save_and_Exit()
'
' Save_and_Exit Macro
' Save changes, close worksheet
'
' Keyboard Shortcut: Ctrl+Shift+X
'
    ActiveWorkbook.Save
    ActiveWorkbook.Close
End Sub
```

Show all macros

Visual Basic code

Show current macro only

Basic steps

1 Display the **Forms** toolbar by selecting **View > Toolbars** and clicking on **Forms**.

2 Click on the button icon (the grey rectangle on the second row).

3 Mark out the position for the button by dragging the pointer over the worksheet.

4 Assign a macro to the button by selecting from the macro list. Click on **OK**.

5 Edit the button name (click on the button text and then replace it with a more suitable name).

Although macros speed up frequently-used operations, the use of the **Tools** menu is not particularly convenient. Adding a command button to the sheet is a very simple process. A macro is attached to the button and then, to run the macro, all you have to do is click on the button. This is a particularly useful approach when setting up macros for other people to use.

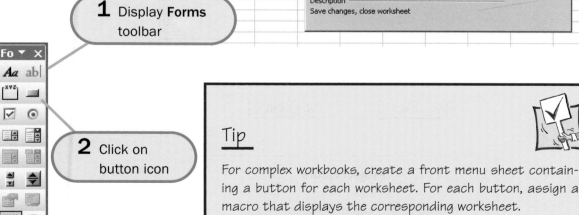

3 Mark button

4 Assign macro

5 Rename button

1 Display **Forms** toolbar

2 Click on button icon

Tip

For complex workbooks, create a front menu sheet containing a button for each worksheet. For each button, assign a macro that displays the corresponding worksheet.

113

Exercises

1   Open the Timesheet.xls file from Chapter 8. Move the chart to a blank area of the Summary worksheet.

2   Create a macro that hides the chart (by hiding the rows or columns behind the chart).

3   Create a macro that shows the chart again.

4   Give the first macro a shortcut of **[Ctrl]+[Shift]+[H]** and select **[Ctrl]+[Shift]+[S]** for the second.

5   Display the macros in the Visual Basic Editor. Edit the macros to increase the number of rows hidden.

```
Timesheet.xls - Module1 (Code)                              _ □ ×
(General)                    ▼    ShowChart                       ▼
    Sub HideSheet()
    '
    ' HideSheet Macro
    ' Hide chart sheet
    '
    ' Keyboard Shortcut: Ctrl+Shift+H
    '
        Rows("22:40").Select
        Selection.EntireRow.Hidden = True
    End Sub
    Sub ShowChart()
    '
    ' ShowChart Macro
    ' Show chart sheet
    '
    ' Keyboard Shortcut: Ctrl+Shift+S
    '
        Rows("21:41").Select
        Selection.EntireRow.Hidden = False
        Range("A20").Select
    End Sub
```

6   Add buttons to the worksheet for each of the macros.

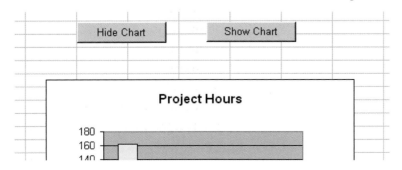

Index

N

Names, 34
   in formulae, 35
Negation, 32
Negative numbers, 33
New Comment button, 26
New files, 12
Normal style, 75
Number formats, 58
Numbers
   as text, 18
   entering, 31
Numeric data, 17

O

Office Assistant, 11
Operators, 30
   arithmetic, 32
   conditional, 40
   logical, 41
Orientation, 102
Overhead projections, 98

P

Page breaks, 106
Page numbers, 102
Page order, 105
Page set-up, 102
Paper size, 102
Parentheses, 33
Passwords, 73
Patterns, 70
Percentages, 32, 60

Pie charts, 89
Point size, 68
Points, 68
Precision as displayed, 61
Preview, 106
Print area, 105
Print options, 107
Print preview, 106
Print quality, 102
Print titles, 105
Printing worksheets, 107
Protecting data, 73

R

Raising to a power, 32
Ranges, 22
   copying, 43
   moving, 45
   multiple blocks, 23
   printing, 107
   totalling, 36
Redo options, 21
References, 44
Regional Settings, 63
Relative references, 44, 110
Replace option, 53
Right-aligned text, 66
Rounding, 61
Row height, 49
Rows, 4
   deleting, 51
   hiding, 52
   inserting, 50
Running Excel, 2

Worksheets
- deleting, 82
- inserting, 82
- loading, 9
- moving, 83
- multiple, 78
- new, 80
- printing, 107
- renaming, 8, 79
- saving, 6
- size, 4

Wrap Text option, 67

X

XLS extension, 7

Z

Zoom value, 23